LOOKING FOR LADY [

A punk rock mystery

By Johnny Angel Wendell

PROLOGUE

PROLOGUE

I guess I just got tired of people suggesting I write a book.

So I did.

End of prologue.

I jest. Musician's stories do tend to all run together blurry-wise with the themes of disaster, breakdowns, industry screw-jobs, furtive sex, lousy pay, drugs, ecstatic joy in moments separated by weeks of tedium—you know. If you've heard one war story you've heard them all and "This Is Spinal Tap" said it all better than anyone else ever could.

Also, every middle aged dude or chick that ever owned a leather jacket and fancied themselves a muso has likely banged out a variation on this already. Math being what it is, there's a lot more behind us than ahead and so summing it up is cathartic. Healthy and free psychotherapy, who could be pissed off at that? On the other hand, who'd really want to read it that much, either.

None of the bands I played in were household names outside the Route 128 belt or maybe in the annals of record collectors. So a memoir would be about as necessary to the world as a third testicle on me.

So, this labyrinth of a yarn is set as a sort of nail biter as opposed to a dewy-eyed reminiscence of a misspent post-adolescence. It is set in the Northeast at the end of the first Punk wave for the most part, so if you ever hung out at CBGB or the Rat (in the east) or Bookie's or La Mere Vipere or the Mabuhay or Masque or Bird or Roxy/100 Club (elsewhere), you may just get a little moist in the corners of your wrinkled eyes reading descriptions of those hoary scenes. I doubt it though—accuracy being a big priority here means that what romance there is here is between people and not for the time or places.

I wrote "Looking For Lady Dee" in about a month. Not saying this to impress you with my warp speed blasts of streams of consciousness but to let you know that this was really an easy task. Because it's fun to just kick out the verbal jams and when the main subject is a part of your life you really don't think about much, when you do, it's amusing. Especially with the colorful crew of characters that populated my life and these pages —I hope you enjoy my recollections of them as much as I did hanging out with them.

Even the invented ones. In fact, they're the best of all—imaginary friends for grownups!

So, by way of dedication, to all of the rock and roll groups I spent my early to mid-twenties with, much love to you---Real Kids, DMZ, Willie Loco, Nervous Eaters, Reddy Teddy, the Atlantics, LaPeste, Neighborhoods, UnNatural Axe, GG Allin, Maps, Human Sexual Response, The Girls, Boys Life, Outlets, DC Tenz, Rubber Rodeo, Classic Ruins, Mission of Burma, Wild Stares, Dangerous Birds—oh, there are so many, please don't be cross with me if I forgot. And the NYC groups, too.

But mostly, this is dedicated to my long suffering family—my wife and two sons and I live in a two bedroom with no office and they were shushed enough in four weeks to last a lifetime. Mostly, this is for them—Amy, Xerxes and Zaz.

And for the indispensable help I got from Tom Carson and Robin Vaughan Kolderie as per just doing it.

And to Suzanna Mars, without whom this never would have occurred to me at all.

And to Janiss Garza, Bruce Haring and most of all, Tracey Ranuaro, who laid the thing out, did the artwork and was bossy when called for.

And to Dee Dee, Johnny, Tommy and Joey Ramone, Johnny Thunders and Jerry Nolan, Stiv Bators and the brothers Asheton—without them, I'd never have been here in the first place.

Here we go. 2/3's of the Great American Novel. As I am an American and this is a novel.

LOOKING FOR LADY DEE

Johnny Angel Wendell.

Chapter 1/Boston/August 1979.

The AC is dead, the air is like paste and if I didn't have a show to play tonight, I'd just as soon lie in a tub of ice—face it, man, summertime in Boston is like ten weeks inside a marathoner's armpit. The humidity hangs over the city like a rotting jellyfish and me, Mr. Johnny Angel, I wilt. The hurried, harried "got to get there now" gait that the locals sport during the rest of the year slows to a dull plodding trudge, too. There's no relief at night, either--all nighttime is, is a darker version of the same swampy murk. In other words, it is a literal steaming bowl of chowder-like suck.

At least it's our city for these few months and the pestilence we call "college students" won't descend on our soggy asses until after Labor Day. The downside to this sitch is that the gigs aren't as jammed as they'll be in September. Them I don't miss, their cash, I miss. Today's starvation, I won't miss. The other day, I pulled a tenner out of the gutter on the Riverway just sitting there and at first I thought it was a crinkled parking ticket that fell off a windshield. Glad to be wrong because I was able to break an involuntary two day fast and believe me when I tell you that greasy Chinese chicken wings from that dump on

Jersey Street when you haven't eaten in two days are pure heaven. This "sort of hit by the Neutron Bomb" emptiness in the streets makes you feel like you own the place a little or at least took it back, everything evens out.

So, my "anticipation-o-meter" is probably set somewhere in the middle for tonight's set at this relatively new joint downtown on Batterymarch called "The Space" It's a dusky, musty, wooden-floored loft second story up, likely was a sweatshop years back. I can picture rows of grim faced immigrant women in babushkas sewing away back in 1910 where we goofball Bohemians now pogo. It might have been a dyke bar recently, too. (the lady that booked us there was so inclined, you see), but it has a nice if rickety stage and being where it is, not too many bridge and tunnel types compared to our other regular haunts. Only ever seen it jammed once when a rumor was afoot that Elvis Costello was gonna sit in with some local band (probably started by that band whoever they were, hats off to 'em for the scam) and all the New Wave rubber-necked collegiate types were in full crane hoping for ole pigeon-toed four-eyes to grace them with his surly presence. He didn't (I was there, my date demanded it. EC's OK by me but not enough to rouse my presence among gawkers, oh, the things we do for love or at least sex).

My gut is doing a mini-rhumba as the sun goes from yellow to evening fireball. "Stage fright" I don't get, but "stage excitement" I do. I just can't wait to "front the roar", as it were—that messy clang that is my band, Thrills. Thrills has existed a few years now and is the center of my modest existence. Probably because the band and the noise it generates is the only thing that's ever shut my overactive brain down from its routine of second guessing and analyzing every little thing in the universe. The ricochet of half heard phrases and half-baked ideas battle each other for space up there in my head and the only thing that shuts off the noise is the sweet pounding that the four of us put out. Oh, and oceans of alcohol too, and I hope most of that is free tonight. The Space has been a little stingy with the spirits last few gigs. Oh well—I gotta clean up properly before I can face the world again, man with stubble and hangover sweat is not an attractive man to anyone but the most star-struck filly and those aren't exactly the cream of the crop assuming one wants after show companionship.

And facial hair is for hippies. Shit, shave and shower time.

What was that tune "standin' in front of my mirror, combed my hair in a thousand ways", oh yeah the Rod Stewart one, well, that is not me, bucko. From shower to mirror, my do is simple--brush forward into its flat wet mop and then like my kid brother's beagle post bath, shake my head back and forth till it dried. Presto and voila, instant Beatles/Byrds/Ramones head, step outside the closet sized can and into the miserable swamp that is my studio hovel, one big room with a small alcove for a box spring and mattress and on the far side of it a heap of rumpled punk rock satori in little hills like leopard skin moguls on a ski trail. A dresser sits empty and lonely near the door, and the fridge could be a reverb chamber--in my thinking, if I keep food in it, I'll eat all of it at once, so barren it stays.

Yeah, I'm not exactly a fussy little diva or a gourmand, either. I wear what's around and eat what I can afford, that is to say when I can afford to eat at all. I'm a skinny but not wiry, pallid and proud son of the suburbs, and just finding anything looks all right on me is a challenge because despite being just five foot eight, I have long, gangly monkey arms and spatula-like fingers, not to mention a pair of humongous flat feet that make me look like the letter "L" in profile, an L with a surly, pouting mug pasted atop it from careful study of his unsmiling heroes like Pete Townshend, Johnny Thunders or Joe Strummer.

Amid the wreckage of my wardrobe is one semi-plausible pair of pegged black Levi's and a low-neck black sheer top that was probably meant for a woman but seems to hang on me all right. No statement of androgyny or asexuality here, it looks good. The jeans do too, even if they're completely worn out at the underside of my hips and ass and split accordingly. As I haven't worn a pair of underpants since I was maybe 16 (in some ways, the hippie and punk things overlap in the positive, at least in a fashion or comfort sense), this would be a problem were I so concerned of flashing a visible penile rig to the assembled-- once again, no statement here, it feels good and looks all right, at least as far as I can tell.

I don't have to tell you that dusting and vacuuming have never existed in this "shanty on the Fenway", right? What I should tell you is that no matter how many times I air it out, the miasma of pesticide, that sickening, sweet smelling, feels like cancer in my nostrils waft is always there and worst in summer. I might feel a little indignant about it, but the last few flats I overnighted in around here all of them had that same eye watering, death to bugs scent about them—and I suppose I didn't have to tell you that, too.

Well, I just did. At any rate, it's us, Thrills and our equally demented peers Unnatural Axe this Saturday, which means all our regulars will be there, Pinky Leather, Mushroom-Head, Pee-Wee, Theo-Logical, Joanie, Gappy, the whole crew of hopping cretins plus the Axe's people, what am I saying, they're the same. Every so often I wish I didn't know the first few rows of shaking heads and hips by name and that blazing strangers with the relentless waves of noise would be a whole lot better but having played to rooms of people unfamiliar with the drill and repertoire already, I like the warm comfort of a loving audience.

On with the shredded black Chucks and down the three flights of stairs (our elevator positively reeks of death trap, so claustrophobe that I am, I avoid it like it was the draft in 1967) and off to the corner to wait for Mike, drummer, van owner and not really thrilled (no pun) chauffeur to get me, swing around the corner and fetch bassist Merle and singer Barb. 75% of the band lives within a block of each other in the Fens, the landfill/swamp section of the city that houses, three blocks away, the Sox. You can even see into Fenway Park from the roof, which I found out one evening whilst banging my upstairs neighbor lady there--she couldn't get off unless she was outside. I obliged, naturally.

My corner, of Queensbury Street and Park Drive, is directly across from the Victory Gardens, the city's biggest cruising strip. I've been propositioned a few times by the gay lads a few times and I could never understand what they saw in me until I realized that the punk rock skin tight jeans ensemble with strategically placed holes was a big ole turn on for 'em. Naive I may be but insane I am not, I stay on my side of the drive after dark 100% of the time---the Boston PD hauls dead dudes out of that morass on a monthly basis and the owner of the local gay bar, the 1270, told me that even as a Vietnam combat vet himself, he'd never venture into those thickets himself. Luckily, Mike's on time tonight, with his beaming and adorable red-headed girlfriend Sandy and into the back I go.

A couple minutes later, we're joined by the other half of our punk-pop ensemble, Barb and Merle. The former is my partner in running the operation, the group's tiny, large-breasted, Darlene Love sounding lead singer and my best friend when we're not trying to kill each other. The latter is the heart and soul of the band, an amiable, affable, balding and bespectacled quipster that plays the bass with a pick, plonking away--this has to be mentioned because on guitar is me, no pick, strumming as if a loud banjo and often mocked for this unorthodox style.

The drive to the joint is maybe 15 minutes but within seconds our ridiculous band's twisted argot--nicknames for every and anyone, code expressions to indicate an uncool audience or audience member we may see and generally the barometer is how "red" they are (as in red necked)--is flying back and forth inside the walls of the van like paper airplanes when teacher's out of the room. There are too many of these to write down, really and Thrills' idiom couldn't be anymore offbeat than anyone else's, but I was once told by a member of some band that was playing with us at the Rat one night that what his group needed was "its own language, like you guys".

Better songs too, I thought, but I responded more politely than that ("stay together long enough and you will"), which was rare--I am one proudly blunt motherfucker that speaks his mind without reservation. Mix that in with the generally prodigious alcohol intake and you have one instant asshole--which I can't deny.

OK, we get to the club and amble up this grimy stairway to the bar. Stage guy sends the freight elevator shambling down the side so we can load in. No boss-lady in sight which means no drink tickets and in my brain, no problem, the Angel charm will work on whatever bartender is (wo)maning the deck this evening. Unfortunately, my school-mate Terry is the drink-slinger in question and immune to my lash-batting she is, which sends the presently flat broke Angel away muttering all the way to the dressing room. The Axe has done their first set and the place is maybe 2/3's loosely full, but the cheap fucker that owns it has clearly kiboshed the AC and so the walls are sweating that condensation thing and the smell of disinfectant plus perspiration and puke and hot wet August air is nausea ignition in full effect. I have places to be and things to do and I don't notice it unless I'm thinking about and at this minute, beer-less and pre-stage jumpy, I'm not. The others are equally jazzed if not juiced, I can tell because Mike and Merle are drumming their fingers along the sides of their legs and Barb's nodding sagely to the last notes of "Orgasm Addict", I guess the DJ thinks this would be a good walk on tune for us.

Set up and plug in time. I got my beat to death sunburst Strat set at below penis level so that I strum straight down as the downbeat kicks in hard on this surfy/poppy opener "Wait For Me" and off we go. First sets are kind of like the beachhead, this is where you establish position for the second one, a few of the lighter songs pepper the performance but at nearly two years in, we got this drill down. I got my thing that I do, this pacing, this insistent can't stay still, white boy in a paint shaker back and forth, Merle grimaces and makes the "bass face" like part agony, part hooked trout, Mike slaps the unholy shit out of everything he owns at least every 4 measures and our buxom belter? I can't watch her, because that crazy woman dances against the beat, flailing her arms on the one and three and if I look, I'll lose the pulse and so I keep my ears to the snare and bob my head at 200 beats per minute.

Forty minutes of this distorted boogaloo and we're done. Ms. Promoter Lesbian Lady palms over our freebie ducats and straight to the bar I go, to gets my share right now, what's mine, the harder I come! Man needs alcohol in generous portions and no fool me, I pass on the piss-like tap crap and opt only for the mixed drinks here. Also take a few compliments and bows, which for the former Jonathan Carmen, is the toughest part of any gig. The Johnny Angel character may be a bit of a course and insensitive ruffian but the actual me doesn't think much of himself no matter what anyone says--but I learned to just plain thank people instead of debating my lack of merit or the band's with them. Also at the bar this evening are my friends David and Mike of the band the Neighborhoods and at this point we decide that instead of Thrills doing an encore, they'll join us onstage as this impromptu punk-rock cover band we decide to call "The Crocodiles". Threading my way back to dressing room with them, we run very sparingly over what few songs we can agree upon, like "David Watts" (the Jam version, we ARE kids), "Chinese Rocks" and "Personality Crisis".

The room is buzzing outside, which means the Axe is onstage for set two of theirs and the energy level is palpable. Shit and a good goddamn, man, there is nothing like a second set on a Saturday night, the idea is to create that blissful blast, that "runaway train down a mountain side" momentum that once again shuts off the mind and makes you entirely in that very minute, it's better than cumming when it happens, believe me here, I've done a lotta both.

They're roaring. Like, it's sort of goofy shit on the one hand, with their funny songs and even simpler than our chord changes (one day I demanded they add a fourth chord to one of their songs or else) but they do achieve liftoff, led by my good pal, Richie, an orange haired kid from Dorchester that makes gorilla faces that crack me up and who speaks in a thick Boston brogue about modern art and cinema and reggae and knowingly at that, which makes him seem even more hilarious than even he intends to be.

And the beats get faster and blur and the room is vibrating and damn, there it is--delirium. This is the state Merle talks about when the crowd surges and the band surges and everything teeters so deliciously on the precipice of total chaos which really is the basis of this music and our bands and this wave of frenzy takes Richie out of his generally placid offstage state and into frantic meltdown during their blast-off anthem "The Creeper". His eyes rolling back in his head,

Rich takes it one leap way beyond--why remain onstage when you have to merge and vault that crazy fucker does, head first into the swaying flesh fray and their raised hands flip him over so his combat boots are coming straight down.

On this poor woman's skull.

Yeah--a girl's head. She's Kathei, a brown haired, timid looking chick, the kind that looks like she sits in the back of the classroom terrified to be called on, but who comes alive via rock and roll and its attendant liberating properties. Richie's boots connect with this nice lady's head, and down she goes. You know when a guard drives for a layup and gets fouled hard and sometimes his head hits the parquet? Well, first she gets shoe leather and sole and then the filthy wood floor of the loft and people are scrambling and Phil is shooting the scene with his camera and everything kind of freeze frames as she's helped up and Richie slithers back to the stage to finish with the scene's invocation, "I Wanna Be Your Dog" and no, if you don't know the song, I'm not telling you.

Fuck me with a cucumber, how do you follow that? Well, this ain't show biz (or the Mudd Club or CBGB's) but we do anyway, the surge of room stench and volume and shock remains high enough for us to surf it all the way to our anthem, whose hook is a shouted "Hey!" some twenty times in two minutes flat and the fists fly in unison to it, all the way to Dave and Mike and Merle and I massacring the Dolls and Thunders tunes with gusto and abandon and zero skill. Place empties out slow and steady, only the musicians and bar staff remain, waiting for at least breakfast cash and then some to come out of the office. Fifty bucks a piece---an orgy of geetas!

I'm amped as per always, so when word of an after-hours house shebeen over in Brighton is broached, well, you don't need to have to ask twice. Three AM and thirty or forty grubby twenty something's blaring the Buzzcocks and Culture and Gang of Four yeah, there's beers and what's your name then?

"I'm Diane", giggles this petite, skinny, blonde, kind of preppy-looking little girl. "That was so much fun, you guys are wild".

"Oh yeah, thanks", says Mr Negative Charm himself. "You go to college then?" (Said in a snarky and semi-dismissive tone to establish me as the bad boy and her as nice girl, I mean, "role playing"? Nah, just acting naturally, as Buck or Ringo might say). I so love these clean ones. They always reveal the most when you're kissing them or sucking or splitting them, like you've opened up a chamber of happiness in them, like a lilac tree exploding its petals. The hardened and jaded scenester girls are fun too, but not challenging or revelatory. They're like taking the bus somewhere as opposed to hitching the ride, predictability wise and with the same loss of discovery and joy. But no matter who you may be, after 3 AM, if you're stag, you're game and probably wanna get off the bench.

Well, approximately twenty minutes hence, Ms Diane and Mr Johnny are boinking away on the lawn next to the place's driveway. Look--mix booze with testosterone and add excited female with the traditional roles reversed of man hunts woman becoming woman hunts man and there will be spontaneous fucking. I'm sure at MIT there's a formula for this. At any rate, the damned Massachusetts summer heat is still cranking at four AM and upon that sweet little belly of hers, there's a little puddle of Johnny and Diane sweat, which she comments upon and in a rare moment of sexual chivalry, I brush off her. One of her friends interrupts the proceedings and asks if we want to leave and we repair to the punk rock crash pad on Queensbury to resume the shagging until sunrise. No morning uncomfortableness, too. No debating whether or not to ask for her number or to be deflated when she clearly doesn't want an encore or a proper date herself. Boy sated, girl sated, everyone wins and Diane gives me a little wave goodbye as she shimmy/bunny-hops out my door.

I'd say it was a good gig.

But it got better.

Four days later, Richie calls me up. "Hey man, you remembuh that knockout thing at the Space, with Kathei, when I landed on her 'ead?"

"Yeah?"

"Well, she called Albert on TBS (WTBS, college punk rock station) and told him that she'd had a brain tumuhh--a fuckin' tumuhh in her 'ead".

"No shit?"

"No shit, Johnny. Anyway, when she went in for them to look at it yesterday, they couldn't find it-- they think I kicked it right out of her 'ead!"

"No shit?"

"No shit! I can't believe it--I mighta saved her life-- by kicking her 'ead in!"

"That's really cool, man", I say. "Her life was saved by rock and....or whatever it is you play".

"Hahahahahah".

"See ya later, Monk".

Damn, summer's over soon. Wonder what's coming in the fall besides the fuckin' interloper BU kids. Guess I'll find out pretty soon.

Chapter 2/Facebook/Cyberspace/August 2013.

VIVDeMILO: Hey!

JOHNNYANGELWENDELL: Hey?

VIVDeMILO: How are you?

JOHNNYANGELWENDELL: Peachy keen--and who might you be?

VIVDeMILO: I'm Vivienne from Boston. Are you the Johnny Angel that used to be in Thrills?

JOHNNYANGELWENDELL: The same.

VIVDeMILO: Cool. I used to check you guys out all the time.

JOHNNYANGELWENDELL: And now you want your money back?

VIVDeMILO: Oh, goodness no, nothing like that— is this a bad time?

JOHNNYANGELWENDELL: No, I'm just playing.

VIVDeMILO: Oh, well I quite liked your band.

JOHNNYANGELWENDELL: Great. What's up?

VIVDeMILO: Do you remember a girl from the punk scene named Dee McClain?

JOHNNYANGELWENDELL: Of course.

VIVDeMILO: Oh, good. Dee was my best friend in the scene. We used to come and see you.

JOHNNYANGELWENDELL: Oh yeah? You want your money back?

VIVDeMILO: Pardon?

JOHNNYANGELWENDELL: Joking. Dee was a character. I had some seriously intense ups and downs with her but she kinda vanished. Have you heard from her, I know she isn't here on FB, I checked.

VIVDeMILO: No, I haven't heard anything in thirty years from her and lately I've been thinking about her, you know how that is. I thought maybe you might know something.

JOHNNYANGELWENDELL: Yeah, I know that feeling. I think she went totally straight and probably married some rich dude in upstate New York or some such shit, that's where she's from, y'know? Like, put the "I am a bad girl" costume away and decided that "suburban matron" was more to her liking and comfort.

VIVDeMILO: Yes, I thought that too but she's not listed anywhere up in Rochester, I googled all kinds of names and her parents old address, nothing.

JOHNNYANGELWENDELL: I lost track of her maybe in '82, I went to her place in Chelsea and left her a note, never heard back.

VIVDeMILO: Yes, that was her last address.

JOHNNYANGELWENDELL: Place was a shithole a roach motel. Probably goes for three grand a month now if it isn't a condo. LOL--fuckin' New York City.

JOHNNYANGELWENDELL: Why the sudden interest if you don't mind me asking, Viv?

VIVDeMILO: I just can't stop thinking about her because we were so close and then she moved to New York and went kind of crazy and then disappeared. It just seems bizarre or preposterous that she would disappear completely without a trace.

JOHNNYANGELWENDELL: What do you mean by kind of crazy? I saw her in Manhattan, we played down at Hurrah and CB's and she was there at Hurrah, we hung out and had a great time, didn't seem crazy.

VIVDeMILO: She never told you about what she was doing then.

JOHNNYANGELWENDELL: Nursing school, yes?

VIVDeMILO: She started in nursing school in Boston. New York, I don't know. I guess she didn't want to put you off, she was always talking about you.

JOHNNYANGELWENDELL: Like what was she up to besides having black hair and being more punk rock in New York, do you know?

VIVDeMILO: Hang on phone.

JOHNNYANGELWENDELL: K

VIVDeMILO: Editor---I have to take this--brb?

JOHNNYANGELWENDELL: Whenever.

VIVDeMILO: We can talk later, really.

JOHNNYANGELWENDELL: Sure. Do what you gotta do.

VIVDeMILO: Thanks, ttyl.

JOHNNYANGELWENDELL: See ya.

Chapter 3/Los Angeles, CA/my brain/ September 2013.

I couldn't tell you when the first time was when I saw Dee McClain but I never stopped seeing her even when she wasn't there. Especially now after talking to this Viv woman, who I know I musta seen but can't place right at this minute, which makes her like 90% of the people I've encountered. It isn't that they're anonymous or drab, it's just that my brain is saturated at this point with faces and conversations.

That will never happen on the issue of Dee, though. When you play in bands as a kid and encounter so many of them, chicks are like the credits at the end of a movie while being the best part of the movie at the same time. They stream by quickly and you pay them minimum mind except when something about them stands out and is profoundly striking and maybe they become your sweetheart or barring that, a memory that surfaces briefly, makes you pause and then disappears again, like a seal coming out of the ocean and then returning.

Maybe I'm feeling the seal image with Dee because the last time I saw her, she had this slick and shiny mane of dyed black hair. I have one fucked up association process.

But the first time I did see her, she didn't look like that at all, because that's what all the punk rock chicks you'd see back in the day did, dip into the dye pots. Barb did, with that damaged red shag of hers and whenever a platinum head was bobbing up and down (whether dancing or in your lap), you knew Mother Clairol had made its score. The Manic Panic thing was a bit down the pike, except in the New York scene.

Dee, no. She was this angelic little thing on first glance, natural blond hair with this mathematically perfect part down the middle, a little bit of powder and lipstick but oh so subtle which I'm sure was the style in whatever town she came from. Her teeth were straight and normal, too but not like that piano key, pearly perfect post braces thing that suburban kids have, they were just right and you could tell because she smiled mouth wide open, also not too punk rock when a smile was a sign of adjustment and happiness and ''we can't have any of that as we're the blank generation'' or whatever internalized bullshit that wave of kids felt they had to front as. Dee never seemed to bother with that initially. Her evolution in New York was when she went whole hog anti-social. While socializing with other nihilists—Lou Reed was right, those were different times.

Dee seemed like one of those "horse girls", you know--an equestrian. Not like she ever said she camped out at a barn but it wouldn't have surprised me in the least if her folks bought her a palomino or something and that all of her summers were spent there and grooming "Silky" or "Dasher", no that's a reindeer's name, oops. I have no idea if that was the case with her as it never came up when we met or afterwards. But she was a lot like the chicks I grew up with in Wellesley, the little town I grew up in. Generally, I didn't talk to them unless they were peer girls, people like me, the stoner outcasts. Dee, on the other hand could have been that jerk-off fantasy mother lode herself--the cheerleader!

If so, she wore it well (another Rod Stewart reference....) and it made a distinct impression on me. This was probably not lost on the other girls in the cadre of Boston's punk second wave, if I hadn't just heard from her friend Viv, I'd think Dee probably had no female friends back then at all. She stood salient or so I remember her that way.

Not the case with her and the dudes. Needless to say, when fresh meat is tossed into the cage of the crazed post-adolescent brat musician and it's of an exotic species, the horns come out and the ram-bucking begins. Forget candy and flowers or even good drugs, excepting cash money itself, psychotic male attention is the hottest aphrodisiac of them all. Not only did Dee first date our first bass player, a shag haired metal fan that was Mike's friend from high school and lasted 4 months in the band, but after him, my friend David and then a few of the older cats. She was very much in demand and by the kind of "bad boy" that I think she craved.

But that smile, that smile of hers--that's what killed me, even more than her taut, pert little ass (thank you, Silky?). If you didn't really see it (the smile, not the ass), it was a nice, almost polite grin, a "pleased to meet you, governor" type middle to high society smile. But because it came with her eyes, two deep brown gun-barrels pointed right at the center of your skull, you knew that she was simmering, maybe even burning a little, to not be so imbued with politesse but perhaps to kick against the proverbial pricks and perhaps nestle in the gutter for a spell, which was likely why our first encounter was at the Rat and not at a cotillion.

The goddamned Rat. Boston's CBGB. The legendary birthplace of New England punk rock. Oh how many pages of internet-based weepy prose have been churned out by middle agers about that basement heap like it was the Cavern come back to life and relocated from Liverpool to Kenmore Square. Indeed, it was a bizarre little place and if it hadn't been seediness central it wouldn't have been the same. But when people romanticize the joint with Taj Mahal type rhapsodies, you know their selective amnesia has done kicked in.

First of all, there were two levels, the street level bar, which was more or less a typical anonymous watering hole of the Boston University type, BU is but a few blocks went on Comm. Ave. The Rat itself, housed in the general Rathskellar, was downstairs to one's immediate left as one went through the door. Right around the time I first laid eyes upon Dee, there was a new doorman, a large, imposing, neatly suited man with a regal, leonine face and brillo-like white-fro. I would come to know him over the years as Mitch, a former jazz sax player that nearly fainted in surprise when I correctly ID-ed a tune on one of his tapes (with him wailing) as "All the Things You Are".

I ain't quite as narrow as I appear. Mitch and I were friends almost immediately and remained so until the day I moved to California, which was the last time I saw him. After the band started playing there and making them money all the time in the late 70's, the cover charge disappeared for me and so I'd be waved in to make the fast left turn down threadbare stairs and into the Rat itself, which is not unlike descending into the hull of the world's smelliest galleon.

CBGB's floor was legendary for the piles of its owner's dog-shit everywhere and it was like negotiating a fecal minefield there but the Rat's floor had its own completely repellent patina, the carpet, presumably red when laid was spotted black with enough chewed wads to suggest a gum-chomping championship has been held there, this and butts ground into the lung-wrecking fibers. The bar was long and worn, with two or three gents manning the taps and only a complete doofus would ever drink what came out of them, I think they'd last been cleaned out during the Eisenhower Administration. Rat beer was such a pungent brew that it was said that you could smell it coming out of the pores of whomever you woke up next to in the morning.

Down past the bar was a pool table soon to be removed as the club became a big deal to fit in more bodies and to its left, the stage. Modest and moderate the PA was, but big enough to handle we of the inept yet loud set and so the actual sound there was fairly professional--even if the pay and its dubiousness via the club's staff wasn't.

One never got anywhere near the pay that one thought they ought to, no matter how many people one brought in. Some enterprising bands like the Ramones would station their manager at the door to make sure they got what was coming to them but we never had that luxury. Plus, we didn't really want to enrage either the owner, a walrus-mustachioed, white haired character named Jim that never said a word to me which I took as a sign to button my lip or else around him (as there were but two places to play, really) or to set off his enforcers, the club's Brobdinagian crew of toughs, the notorious Rat bouncers.

Dee and I likely met on a weeknight early in Thrills' career. Our dream was not the Garden or Orpheum but to become a weekend headliner-- record deals went to older, mystical acts like the Talking Heads (who I saw as a trio at the Rat), the Ramones, our friends the Cars or all the English groups. Our goals were more modest--work ones way up to headlining a Thursday and then, if all went well, a weekend.

No, I don't remember the day but I remember the Dee the first time as if a photo album. Walking off the stage in spring 1978 to a more or less empty club (I was not yet jaded, so empty was better than not onstage or at home with the horrible woman I cohabited with), there she was in her skintight red top and blue jeans, flared at the ankle bell-bottoms. The metamorphosis into Deena Is A Punk Rocker had not yet begun.

"Hey, that was kinda cool", she said to me as the mop sweat off my coif burned into my eyes. "Are those all your songs?"

"Yeah, I wrote 'em," said Señor Standoffish. As fine as she was, I had begun to hone the persona into a very successful act. Be all sullen and James Dean damaged at first, then kinda/sorta open up a little and then boyish if hostile charming. This made the women of the day feel very special, as if they had finally gotten through to the troubled juvenile delinquent. Praise the spirits there was no texting then or I'd have been busted on my third groupie. That and the evidence of a live in girlfriend although through the groupie grapevine, I was already well known as a lad whose commitment to monogamy was dental floss-thick on my best day.

"Well, they're good, ya know, different--you guys play here a lot?" she asked.

"When we can".

"Yeah, I'd like to check you out again. What's your name?"

"Johnny Angel".

Huge grin, that gorgeous, genuine, adorable, unselfconscious smile like the happiest croc in the marsh.

Hands on hips and with an "I do declare" head-tip, she said "It is not, your mom did not name you Johnny Angel. Where did that come from?"

"This girl I used to see lived up on top of that hill on Comm. Ave and I'd walk up to see her and my cheeks got all red and so she called me that and I guess it stuck", I said. (Also complete crapola, I named myself Johnny Angel, but sometimes a good myth bears beating to death).

"Well, Johnny Angel, I am Dee McClain and I'm happy to meet you". And she stuck out her hand and I kissed it and she smiled that damned smile again and gave forth with a gauzy "oh my, what manners, Mr Angel".

Then she remarked that she had to split to get up for nursing school in the morning, effectively icing plan A for me.

"I'll see you again, huh?" she asked.

"Sure--just check the Boston Phoenix and see when we're playing again, I'll see you then". She thrusts and I parry--no head over heels give it all away signal from the budding pro JA.

And I watched her as she went off into the night, up those creaking stairs into the noise of the street, that perfect ass ascending away from me.

Thanks, Silky.

Chapter 4/Facebook/Cyberspace/September 2013.

VIVDeMILO: Hey, you there?
JOHNNYANGELWENDELL: I'm not all there, I here. Not I hear. Old musician. Deaf.
VIVDeMILO: LOL!
JOHNNYANGELWENDELL: LOL--what's new in yr world?
VIVDeMILO: Working, ssdd.
JOHNNYANGELWENDELL: Yeah? You never told me what you did.
VIVDeMILO: Photographer.
JOHNNYANGELWENDELL: Where at?
VIVDeMILO: The sprawling cosmopolitan city of Jacksonville, Florida.
JOHNNYANGELWENDELL: Impressed. Nauseated but impressed, never been, I shouldn't badmouth it.
VIVDeMILO: Be my guest, it is bloody dreadful.
JOHNNYANGELWENDELL: Why there?
VIVDeMILO: Prices out of San Fran and family in FL.

JOHNNYANGELWENDELL: "Priced out", you mean?

VIVDeMILO: Yes, typo. Was there ten years, print dried up, I do general photography here, events.

JOHNNYANGELWENDELL: Last thing you did?

VIVDeMILO: Bodybuilding thing. Verrrry freaky, Johnny.

JOHNNYANGELWENDELL: Yeah? You meet all the muscle dudes?

VIVDeMILO: Yes. They're weird, I do this shoot every year, same guys. Strange subculture.

JOHNNYANGELWENDELL: They hit on you all macho n shit?

VIVDeMILO: No, never. Maybe all that stuff they take makes them sort of neutered?

JOHNNYANGELWENDELL: Makes em huge for sure.

JOHNNYANGELWENDELL: Cool. So wut up?

VIVDeMILO: I want to find her.

JOHNNYANGELWENDELL: Dee?

VIVDeMILO: Yes.

JOHNNYANGELWENDELL: You checked regular places, Social Security, Yahoo people search, all that?

VIVDeMILO: Yes. Nothing.

JOHNNYANGELWENDELL: OK, family?

VIVDeMILO: Where, how?

JOHNNYANGELWENDELL: Father's name, her mother's?

VIVDeMILO: Father is William. She has brothers, dk names.

JOHNNYANGELWENDELL: Checked father?

VIVDeMILO: Not yet, I wanted to talk to you first.

JOHNNYANGELWENDELL: Yeah? Why?

VIVDeMILO: I'm a little freaked out. Like, do you ever believe it's possible that she didn't want anyone to know where she ended up?

JOHNNYANGELWENDELL: Well, that wouldn't be the first time, right?

VIVDeMILO: That's very true. But even back then, she called. There's no phone anywhere on her.

JOHNNYANGELWENDELL: So, you want me to help you, yeah?

JOHNNYANGELWENDELL: Cause I know nothing, kid. She came and went so long ago, you know?

VIVDeMILO: Do you think I'm crazy for this?

JOHNNYANGELWENDELL: Fuck no.

VIVDeMILO: Good. I mean, that's what I want from you, like not time or anything, just tell me I'm not totally insane.

JOHNNYANGELWENDELL: Maybe a little insane but otherwise I'd have unfriended you!

VIVDeMILO: LOL...OK--I'm going to check the family out.

JOHNNYANGELWENDELL: Keep me posted.

VIVDeMILO: K

JOHNNYANGELWENDELL: See ya

VIVDeMILO: See you later, Johnny.

Chapter 5/Eastern Massachusetts/Mac's shit-box/ February 1977.

Where in the hell are we going and why are we headed downtown? I thought Mackie's place was in Holliston or Hopkinton, one of those towns and yet, instead of going west, we're going east on Storrow Drive, what gives?

Today's our big day. Mackie, JD and myself are gonna jam--on what, who has any idea. JD is guitar, Mackie the drums and me with my best friend's bass subbing on an instrument I am an absolute abomination on. Recently, I was rehearsing with a local singer/songwriter gent named Marc Thor whose tunes tended to have perhaps 4 chords and a tempo change per in them and that was far too complex for yours truly, his nibs, the world's worst bass player. I have good ears--wicked good ones as my peers might say and can plonk out any tune anywhere that I hear. Thing is, the actual playing of said tune is bound to be in Johnny meter and as such, not exactly session level, even if the session in question was the most basic rock.

The other lads, I've never heard them. JD works down the street from me, him doing computer stuff, data entry and me, messenger and theoretically, stockbroker. That one causes instantaneous urination at the Rat when broached in conversation--indeed, like grandfather and father before me, I am licensed to sell securities. Thing is, that would require finding clients, wearing a suit, being straight--getting my Series 7 was about as much commitment as I had. As such, I am the firm's errand boy, a job I began at 13 during the summers. JD and I have lunch regularly together. He's a dour, frizzy haired kid from JP that absolutely worships the Dead Boys, which is fine in my book as I regard them as fairly fantastic (although I did threaten to beat their scrawny singer up at a Rat gig which naturally earned the singer's respect--masochist). Don't know what he plays like but he has good taste, which is most of the battle.

Mackie is a tall, lanky, balding punk rock/garage rock fanatic whose dream gig would be with DMZ if possible--also evidence of great taste as they are the most exciting of the local crews. Boston's MC5 they are with two great guitars and a deranged lead singer that paints his shades over and blindly swings at a triangle (the orchestra instrument) dangling over his head and then falls face-first into the audience. They're also said to be negotiating with Sire, which puts them in the league of the most holy of all bands, the Ramones.

What this "jam" is gonna entail, who knows, but I know what it won't be. The kind I participated in when I was in high school and after, namely twiddling over the changes to "Moondance" or other pseudo jazz, Christ almighty, I am so fortunate no one at the Rat ever saw me widdley-widdleying over "the blues" on my guitar like a very ham-handed version of the presently persona non grata Jerry Garcia. Whew, I sweat bullets of gratitude knowing that in Year One of punk rock, I entered the ranks anonymous and unknown, my love of groups like the Allman Brothers or Derek and the Dominoes long forgotten, all hail the new breed. In reality, most of that was swept aside by the glam bands like Mott and Slade and Bowie and above all others, the New York Dolls. When that blew away, it was impossible to return to hippie and I made due with the Chuck, Buddy and Eddie stew until seeing the Ramones and Talking Heads and the local bands and that sealed the deal--sort of. Up until recently, I split my time between the Rat and Cantone's, the punk clubs and the discos. I love physical music and the relentless beat of the four on the floor, especially the Philly stuff, was just as much tonic to this trooper as the monolithic blare of punk rock.

Was that a mistake to admit? You gotta watch everything you say these days, some of these punk rock "trend-setters" are like Stalinist commies with the rules and all. All I know is that disco is the right cross that seems to have knocked out California soft rock (and punk rock the quick left jab?) and anything that gets the Eagles off the air is all right, even if chunky secretaries and mustachioed used car salesmen in white suits and cheap chains over hairy chests like it. That sensitive, denim shit screws up my biorhythms, disco may not be as great as P-Funk or James Brown but it sure blows doors on "Life in the Fast Lane" or whatever.

We will not be essaying "Get Down Tonight" this afternoon, though, not like I could even play that piss simple bass part in it. In fact, I'd like to know what the eff is up as we are ascending Beacon Hill, it's Sunday, it isn't like there's an open packy here and I know Mackie knows how to get home from Boston, so......

"Where the fuck are we going, man"?

"Going to get Barb, Johnny," replied the jovial Mackie, as he spun the wheel of his boat like Pontiac to the curb.

BARB? Barbara, that midget red-headed, loudmouthed, bragging arrogant pissant from the Rat? Did you eat my body last night and are now shitting me out your ass sideways, HER? What in the fuck for? My eyes have just done a complete spin like they were part of a slot machine and I didn't bother to conceal that either.

"She wants to sing with us," Mackie says, sensing a hint of Angelic dismay as he pulls the keys out of the ignition, or maybe they just fell out, this car is creaky as shit.

Oh, isn't that just the best news of the day--little miss lousy attitude fancies herself the soul, spirit and embodiment of Patti Smith. Needless to say, this doesn't endear me anymore to her as we have never even been civil to each other. She is not merely a know it all, in my estimation, she broadcasts know it all, which offends me down to the core of my skinny little body. Her claim to fame is that she was supposedly the first DJ in America to play "Anarchy in the UK" on the Emerson College station. It's like a calling card, within the first ten minutes of any conversation, it's "I played Anarchy" the same way a survivor of Normandy might talk about 6/6/44. And the way she puffs her dubious role in their ascent to legendary status up, you'd think she was all four

Sex Pistols at once with her self-important air and all.

She arrives, oh Princess would be Patti and plotzes right down in the back next to JD and starts chattering about nothing which only accentuates my rage at her violation of what I thought would be our three chord tree-house/ sausage fest. It is a typically crummy and overcast winter's day in New England. Minus the patina of snow, it is nothing but grayness and bare branches for miles in the burbs where I was weaned. When we actually alight to Chez Mackie (his parents big old gloomy tomb of a house), it's a relief not to be moving or enduring Barb's solipsistic monologue.

Amps and guitars and a mini PA is set up in the living room. Mackie adjusts his drums and then the awkward moment of silence. Not in a prayer of thanks or reflection but all four of us realized at once the vexing quandary that is leering at us-- what exactly are we gonna play for songs?

We don't know anything and I am not about to volunteer "Whipping Post" or "Why Does Love Got to Be So Sad", no fool me. I remain hippie-closeted.

Barb looks at me as I am probably the ringleader of this motley crew and asks "Ramones?"

"Sure", I say. "Blitzkrieg Bop"?

Everyone nods. That one we know. Not even knowing that very simple song being the people we were would be like not knowing how to chew or wipe one's ass. I am the bass player and therefore I am the temporary band's Dee Dee and so I count it off and we negotiate the first part of the song and the chant and then Barb commences to sing.

"They're forming in a straight liiiiine. They're going through a tight wiiiiind. The kids are losing their miiiinds, the blitzkrieg bop".

What in the flying fuck is THIS? She can SING. And not just sort of wave at the notes like a batter does at a knuckleball, she smacks them and sounds exactly like Darlene Love or Ronnie Spector, my favorites.

"Heyyyy ho, let's go, shoot them in the back nowwww". Like Broadway. Broadway Barb. Ethel Merman sings CBGB's--only it's really good and I have my head down and am pounding out the chords on the bass precisely and steadily, because the other two are not. This is one rickety boat in the ocean for two minutes.

It ends. I'm trying not to look at Barb directly because I am a proud little bastard whose face is spattered with eggs and humble pie and I don't mean in the Steve Marriott sense. She's amazing and I, oh how it kills me to say this......am wrong.

That's only one song however and we're here and now what, captain oh captain?

Now we're stumped and it's "Blitzkrieg Bop" again but we can't play that song all afternoon and so the rundown begins--"Search and Destroy" (head shaking from JD), "Chinese Rocks" (same), "No Fun" (Barb nixes, too low), wait, why not "Sonic Reducer"?

JD nods--at last he will straddle Olympus with his gods and strike forth with their sacred anthem. Except that Mackie is not Johnny Blitz and I am not Jeff Magnum the Dead Boys bass player and so the train wreck accelerates by about the end of the first verse into really horrible noise and I don't mean that in the positive, ground breaking and liberating sense, just plain hack, chopper garbage churned into crud by ham-handed horrors. JD, unknown to us, has been up since Thursday on cheap trucker speed white crosses and is getting redder and redder until fully crimson and then explodes, taking his beautiful white SG off his neck and slamming it into his Twin Reverb until it's sub Pete Townshend shrapnel wreckage only

it ain't the Garden, we ain't the Who, we're three horrified bystanders to complete destruction.
The jam is over.

Total silence all the way back to Boston. JD is half proud and half seething that we massacred his hero's great signature song and he his lovely guitar, Barb and I are in complete shock, Mackie has boat in hand and knows better than to offer even a monosyllable by way of commentary. When we get to her digs, I walk her out to her door.

"Hey, you know, I'm not really a bass player, I'm guitar, we should do something for real, make a band--you think?"

"Yeah, that would be cool, call me."

This may actually be something. This winter may not be all blahs after all.

Chapter 6/Boston/March, 1978

When did we last speak, a year and change ago, right? There's no way--no way on earth--I could have imagined that the last 13 months rolled out the way they did. In fact, if you'd told me in advance what the look back of this time would be, I'd have sprained a gonad cracking up.

Shortly after the nightmare that was the Sunday jam where Barb and I discovered that our mutual hatred society was idiocy, we hunkered down to get going. In what could charitably be termed "fits and starts". With us two, fits tend to be the order or the ordure of the day. Through a drummer I'd played one show with (I was the bass player, and I went far crazier onstage than the rest of the band, hence my immediate termination), Barb and I landed our maiden voyage as a paid pair of performers, backed by said drummer and a real bassist. Back on guitar and ready to conquer the universe.

When I hear old comics or singers or actors fondly reminisce about the terrible dumps they paid their dues in, you can tell there's some affection in their tone. I may live to 130 and never speak sweetly about our cherry popping engagement--at the Birdcage, in the Combat Zone.

Unlike the tawdry strip joints, hand job palaces and "burlesque" houses on Washington Street, the Birdcage was a biker's drinking bar that (I assume) had dancers in cages at one time. Whatever is five steps grungier than "dinge-y" is the Cage, it is actually below the bottom rung of the ladder, gig wise. The permanent twilight of the joint, the dust and grime, the long dancers stage where the four of us set up and gamely massacred our unrehearsed repertoire of Stones, Chuck Berry, the Dolls, Sam Cooke (you can't imagine how twisted our "Twisting The Night Away" was) and the unholy "Gloria/Louie Louie/ Wild Thing" triumvirate repeated ad nauseum--it didn't help that we sucked. The grizzled gents too broke from Harley maintenance to spring for drinks with the girls that "mixed" in the neighborhood poon palaces were our indifferent if not somewhat pissed off audience and even getting our wretched 25 bucks per person out of the old coot that ran the joint was a major task. Luckily, our drummer was a career felon named "Wild Johnny" whose disappearance into the mist of shady deals and dope were legend--he spoke their language and somehow secured the ducats.

I bipped out on the last day before our last set, I cracked (ironically, the Modern Lovers tune "She Cracked" was part of our set list) and couldn't take the miserable grind of me and bassist and drummer never on the same beat and out I went-- they actually soldiered on sans guitar (to dope fiends, that twenty plus fins is worth reciting the phone book in Swahili for an hour if that's what it takes). I was not of that mind or affliction and NO MAS! Well, that's what I claimed to Barb after the fact but the reality of the situation is that my level of panic from the humiliating lousiness of us brought on a paralyzing attack of anxiety which wouldn't even let me walk out the apartment door. I've had them since high school and once they pounce on you, they're like a hawk ripping out your flesh, drying your mouth and making your palms sweat and dizzying your brain until you grab onto something—anything, really—and ride them out. As I never know when they're going to assault me, I am always totally unprepared for them as I was at the Birdcage.

After that agonizing fiasco, I told Barb that it was time to get serious--her job as counter-girl at the Rat record store was neither lucrative nor satisfying and if I'd wanted to play in a cover band, I'd join one (not that any would have me). So, we put an ad in the Phoenix and amazingly, got lots of responses for rhythm sections. While most bassists and drummers that rung me were seriously trapped in Aerosmith-land or worse, blues, we did get one pair of guys that liked what we did and so we lammed out to my mom's basement back in Swellesley and once again, the first thing we did was "Blitzkrieg Bop", only these fellows were sharp--much better than I was. Mike and Jeff, from some little town near Rhode Island, Mike serious (at first) and Jeff a little goofy and spacey--I introduced him to Dee at a later gig and they didn't hit it off that well for that reason.

We were born, we were a band, and now we existed. I suggested the name "Thrillhammers" from a routine I'd read about somewhere which climaxed with "grab my thrill-hammer, baby". Barb didn't fancy a group named for a cock, fine--but "Thrills" was OK by her. Especially with the pretext/story that we'd named ourselves after the Clash song "48 Hours" big hook--"48 hours is a 48...THRILLS". Already we were budding public relations experts, well, liars.

And we had a bit of a problem. Genius Johnny had already booked a gig for this group at Cantone's, an Italian restaurant downtown that was a punk club at night, I think the Real Kids or LaPeste had discovered it and talked the owner into having bands. I had sort of won a wager with the owner's son/booker as per the viability of the band the Feelies, who I said would draw no one and I was right (great band, but no one had ever heard of them, even my obscurest/purist posse)--he said he owed me one and the payoff was the unheard and unseen band of mine getting a Thursday night. Thing is, we had no songs. None. And three weeks to come up with two sets to be repeated twice, four sets.

I threw together some truly atrocious songs at the pace of two or three a day that only passed muster if Barb laughed at the lyrics over the phone from my dad's office. Like "Baby, I'm So Lonely I Wanna Be A Nun" and "Tards On Parade" and our first masterpiece "Fun In The Springtime" whose chorus went like this:

"We been kicking cripples/all been kicking cripples/Thrills been kicking cripples/kicking cripples all night long/Barb likes to do it/Johnny likes to do it/Mike likes to do it/Jeff likes to do it/ Kick, kick, kick/We're vicious little no cares/Been tipping over wheelchairs/And if you wave that crutch at me/I'll kick you in the fucking knee".

Roll over, George Gershwin and tell Cole Porter the news, right?

Typically, we'd learn and drill with more focus than I'd ever shown at school or work. One night, we learned this song which had three verses and a bridge and clocked in a 52 seconds. It should have been called "Fun" as that's what its hook was, but that was too dreary and "Funtime" was taken so we debated a title:

BARB: It can't be called "I Like Having Fun", that's weak.
JEFF: Right, yep, weak.
MIKE: Why not "Pork Fried Rice"?
JEFF: Yeah! Pork fried rice!
JOHNNY: How about calling it "Drano Enema"? (Barb nods, Jeff nods, Mike perplexed and outvoted).

Finally, the glorious night, December 15th came and we loaded in gear and PA and nervously waited to show the world our stuff. As Barb was a semi-fixture on the scene and me the class clown, there was a good turnout of night-crawlers and other musicians, all figuring that at least we'd be amusing if not completely atrocious.

We were a bit of both, our first set being about 32 minutes long--15 songs. Commencing with "Rave

Up Tonight" and "Drano Enema" and battering classics like "My Boyfriend's Back" at 300 mph and ending with our ode to wheelchairs tipping over and paraplegic punting, people's jaws dropped--we were literally playing at warp speed with this 60's pop goop smeared over the top like meth laced marmalade. At one point, I looked out to see this bearded fellow doing his fucking homework in the first row--this indignity will not stand, I sauntered over and kicked his table to its side and screamed at him over the din "this isn't the fucking library, asshole".

I don't think he's missed a gig since.

After the set was over, I ambled to where one of my older musician gurus was, a bass player in a popular, tough rock and roll outfit called the Nervous Eaters. He was leering from ear to ear.

"What's so fucking funny?"

"Nothing", he replied. "I think this is my new favorite band". And then he shook his head, took a long pull off his beer and looked me in the eyes.

"Johnny," he said. "You are about to get more pussy that you could ever dream of in your whole life". Big wide, knowing leer.

"You're nuts", I said. "The groupie thing doesn't exist anymore, you old hippie relic--get your head out of Woodstock, maaan".

Six months later, I sheepishly apologized. He had been right, joy of joys.

Three sets later, we collected our 36 dollars and I went back to my crib, somewhat satisfied. Only somewhat because living with me at the time was a woman I could barely stand--I think that like most guys, you get away from mom's house and you glom onto the first willing would be mama. This one was a skinny, hyper-nervous chick that probably thought "smart Jewish boy from Wellesley make good catch". As that description is true and all, it does omit small details like "hates work", "lives in a dream world" and "alcoholism" which all mean that her ideal man and I were far from the same homo sapiens.

So, we're a little tense up there in my odd apartment on Marlborough Street. Especially as it's really only one huge room--probably was the dining room of a brownstone at one time then carved up into units, hell it may have been the servant's quarters, call me Jeeves! So, we were always up each other's nostrils. And that cloying, nagging, violin-string about to snap sounding voice of hers--that alone gave me a perpetual soft-on and I may be the horniest fucker breathing. Plus, her fetish was sewing and there were these horrible patterns strewn all over the place like the corpses of Raggedy Andy and Ann blown to bits in Berlin and the idea that cohabited with a Good "Housekeeping" subscriber didn't exactly jibe with my self-image as Crazy Johnny Guitar Angel.

Rehearsals, therefore, were constant. And the band got a bit better step by step, weaker tunes were getting peeled away but then last month, nature intervened and a river of shit hit a mountain of fan.

Around the first, Boston got slammed with a wet load of snow, maybe a foot and a half that mucked shit up plenty but not to a standstill, it was significant enough to cave the roof of the Hartford Civic in, right? Then deep freeze and a repeat of same, only this time twice as much and everything hit so hard and so fast that the universe stopped moving--you couldn't even see the roofs of parked cars in front of our building. Was like a massive pillow had exploded over Boston with such force that even shoveling out was impossible as there was nowhere to put the snow anyway.

Imagine two or three inches of pure white out per hour--it was like someone had exploded a warehouse of pillows over Massachusetts and millions of feathers took up every inch of space.

Which meant me and misery personified were housebound and unable to avoid each other. And in the world's quickest burst of cabin fever and anxiety anywhere, she could hold in her secret no longer.

"I FUCKED ANOTHER MAN". No, I didn't reply with "come again?"

Thank you so much for informing me of this on the only day of my life when getting out the door was physically impossible--how can I ever repay you?

Turns out, she'd boned her fucking hair stylist, where I didn't ask and I certainly didn't want or need details. In fact, all I could think of was, one straight hairdresser in all of Boston, naturally that's the one that fucks my girlfriend.

I calmed her and assured her it was OK--in fact it was, I didn't mind that much. Child of the early 70's that I am, monogamy seems like way too much energy to enforce as law, make love and lots of it. Maybe she was looking for me to explode and get all macho indignant, but really, all I wanted was for her to stop wailing about it as if she'd massacred a busload of monks with a machete--it was not a big deal. Shit, the month before this massive blizzard and subsequent tearful confession of infidelity, I had rolled and tumbled in this very room with the lovely and vivacious Pinky Leather and neither she nor I gave a second thought as to the ramifications of my ramming her were. (Clever, eh?).

The entire area was in total shutdown. The trains didn't run, the streets were ski-friendly, no traffic in and out of the city which meant that if you were sans supplies, tough shit, laddie, you were sans grub. Luckily, a friend of my dad's lived at the base of Beacon Hill and I skidded over there for a loan that took half a day to get. We ate--generally in silence and then when the sidewalks were at least negotiable, I went to the only place I ever went which was coincidentally the only one open--the Rat.

Like shipwrecked sailors we were, me hearties, us the locals and this stranded band from Michigan, the Romantics. Sixties type stuff and not of the Iggy/MC5 brand, three sets a night of everything they knew and luckily for them, the bar didn't run out of alcohol nor did the willing and chilly females deny the Detroit dandies their affections. Me, I just drank and hung out happy to be away from domestic disturbance in the making, safer at the Rat amid my damaged peers and the deranged staff there, who luckily liked me because otherwise I, with my wise tongue, would have been eviscerated with incredible efficiency by those bouncers--best to stay on the good side of the barbarians when they're at the proverbial gate, yeah?

I'd come home to the woman in her self-pitying stew of self-flagellation and try to assure her I wasn't ticked off at all. But I bet it sat in my payback-craving subconscious somewhere because last week, I returned the favor (minus sobbing admission and meltdown) in our very own bed. With the chick my bass player was seeing on and off no less, Ms. Day McClain.

Yeah--Dee. I was always really into that sly trouble-maker smart arse and I think she and I actually conversed more than she and Jeff did. So, this is what happened, honest truth.

My girlfriend got a job babysitting one of her high school cronies' brats out in the boonies on a Friday night, which meant she'd be staying out there. Dee calls me and says that this band she likes, the Atlantics, were playing BU--I like them too, they're like a raunchier version of the Raspberries, only they wear suits and sort of look like a perverse Freddie and the Dreamers. We took the T over to the student union hall and saw them, they were great and I was pretty happy to have Dee as a date because frankly, I was crazy about her. For all her innuendos and cleverness, there was a warmth under that conflicted exterior that was baby-blanket soothing and I sensed that I was maybe the only person that knew it was there.

After the gig, we came back to my place and not the Rat, which was strange because it was on the way and open and we both loved getting our drink on. Sitting on our bed in the middle of the enormo-studio, we were chatting about band stuff, music, people and I leaned over and kissed her softly on her lips--every tangible circumstance on the earth was against this idea, but it seemed as natural as a jump over a puddle.

She smiled, said nothing and kissed me back. And I ran my hand through her hair and kissed her again and it was heaven, it was pure bliss, it was drug-like. And we laid down next to each other and I ran my hand up under her sweater and that skin was so wonderful, like flawless perfect and she sighed and whispered "I know I'm really small, I hope you don't mind".

I didn't answer, how could I? Her breasts, damn, they were part of her and as a whole, she's magnificent and pristine and in the warmth of our bed against freezing outside, she's destination. I pulled her sweater up and my tee shirt too and touched my chest to hers, nipples to nipples, rolling ever so slowly as I tasted her tongue and ground my hips into hers. Undoing her jeans, I pulled them down in one motion and her little white panties as well and slid my tongue into her navel.

Dee took my face in her hands and held my head for a moment and then, her chin to her chest said that I might not want to go where I was going, that I might not like it. But I slid my tongue down between her legs anyway and onto her tiny clit, which I jabbed with the tip of my tongue and her worries stopped, yes, she started writhing and shaking as I licked and as I stroked her nipples with my free hand.

"Please come up, come up now and fuck me, Johnny", she sighed and I undid my own jeans as I rose and kicked them off, taking her hand to guide me into her. If there had been worry or fear it was long gone, I entered her as she gasped and then rolled her atop me, where she shook those amazing hips hard in a wild buck, almost snapping my cock off inside her. We rolled back to me on top of her, in that perfect motion, that rhythm, that beat that we both rode until I came inside her, jaw and teeth and eyes clenched only to be opened to see her angelic face beaming up at me. We dressed backs to each other but when I turned to see her, she was smiling at me oh so shyly. As if to say that this was all right and natural enough and not rushed or somehow a mistake.

Yeah, I'd be lying if I said it wasn't a little awkward but when I walked her out to her cab, I was sort of tongue tied and still putting up a front, trying to be cool but also trying to get her to understand. I kissed her on her cheek and told her I'd call in the morning and I did and it was half pause and half talk, like we'd crossed into some new territory that was desired but because it was uncharted, tentative like each new word was a baby step into our new world.

Dammit. Sometimes I think it isn't that you want someone to know how you feel, but that you do feel at all.

Chapter 7/Boston/April, 1978.

In a scene populated by and overrun with sleazy, skeevy, scumball creeps and cons, very few were as intestine-twisting vile as Nick Rowland. Ghoul like pallid, with that over soaped and neat Irish Catholic mama's boy sheen all over his scheming yet blank face, he seems like a reasonable even pensive gentleman of refinement until you dig into his activities. Which are as evil and morbid as any slasher flick villain come to life on a midnight movie screen.

Rowland fancies himself as both a musician of the dark poet variety and a Svengali to young up and coming musicians. In reality, he is a 5th rate Lou Reed worshiping poser of the worst kind and his interest in the art of younger players tends to begin and end at their conquest and bedding. By young, I mean underage and by younger players, I mean males. Nick is a garden variety chicken-hawk.

You can't swing the corpse of a cat in this fucking city without striking a predator ped. It's the ugliest little secret everyone knows, the prize in the Cracker Jack Box of kid abuse--that damaged glaze over so many young people's eyes isn't the sting of rain and snow.

Ain't nobody talking because nobody's got to say anything. It's as understood as the Winter Hill Mob or payoffs to cops.

I had auditioned for one of Rowland's groups while I was still shacking in my mother's suburban crib. And knew nothing of him, for all his bluster and bravado and tireless self-promotion, he was less known to the general public or me than a Red Sox batboy. We were lined up on a bench at some church one afternoon, a gaggle of guitarists all waiting to play the same two tunes, in a row. Running the proceedings was a tough little street kid that got slight giggles every time he moved us along, he was the stage manager, you see, and couldn't have been more than 15. The giggles were because he was supposedly Nick's "companion".

I remember little of the jam, it was tedious and I was no more interested in them than they of me and I forgot all about him until Thrills started playing the same club circuit a few years later. By now, his companion is playing and leading one of our peer groups. And clearly chafing and uncomfortable in this role, it's one thing to do what you don't wanna do to get by as a hustler, it's another when you're approaching mainstream main-street and wanna be what you are as opposed to a pervert's bauble. The other option used to be the pavement and abject poverty.

Rowland, however, claims to be a band manager--so he says. Colonel Tom Pedophile. I joke, but I think because the old sicko could get bookers on the phone and probably gives kids in the band a place to rehearse, they allow this grotesque symbiosis to remain. And he'll stand at the side of whatever stage they played on, radiant with glee--he is a powerful man. Just ask him. Ask anyone else and they'll tell you he's a hanger-on at best which makes him more or less anyone with a fantasy and his are grotesque.

I guess you've gathered that I hate the vulture. You're wicked smaht, pat yourself on the back.

But at this point in time, he is losing his grip. As punky pop is becoming more palatable to the masses, the college kids are no longer lapping up ethnic snazz like blues or reggae like they had. And the band he followed was developing a sound and a following, like us, they were dropping their derivative slabs of the stupid and getting catchier and stronger. And needing this bunged up old monster less and less every month. Not like they did anyway, I think they regarded him as a nuisance that wasn't worth shedding.

Like the other members of our core of "second wave bands", I always go see them if I wasn't playing or be sure to see them when they were playing with us. We hang together, it is better than high school, man--I was always a shoe-staring, undersized introvert back in my teens as were Richie and David and Peter and the rest of us, but our lives were lit up by this new thing to the point where we all didn't just blossom, we exploded, free of the constraints and repression of the neat little lace curtain towns we were raised in. And so it is for the people that come to see us too, reborn into what they wanted to be away from the carefully molded model of parental wishes, the boys threw away their he man/adult affected personas, the girls smeared on lipstick and powder and paint to maybe exaggerate their features instead of pinking them up---the gender bending we'd loved in glam had resurfaced as not so much a puckered kiss but as a spit in the eye to a culture that sells the same mind-numbing mantra of sameness to anyone not willing to punch back at it.

Yeah I wax poetic, so fuck me, right? I finally feel like I belong to a club that not only has me but won't have people I don't wanna see, the jocks and their giggly molls. Not always though--the energy and movement of our circle does draw the unsavory types like Rowland who are even worse than the squares and straights--at least they're made nervous by what we represent, that douchebag sees only cock, balls and dollar bills.

So I expect to see that bony fingered crone at tonight's gig. I also expect to see Dee McClain as she sometimes dates the singer of the other band and after all, I will be there too. She and I have been keeping the deal on the simmer lately, it's the big gorilla in the room that we fucked and all, she seems to have hooked up with my friend and I am at best semi-happy for them, because, big surprise, I wish it was me and not him.

It ain't. On the bright side, it transpires that Dee loathes Rowland as much as I do because the old mean queen is especially *vicious* to Dee and not like he's gonna hit her with a flower, right (OK, I'll stop with the song references--briefly). Rowland, for all his pretend business savvy and bad acting job botch of being "detached and professional" is seeing his prize stable slipping away, with Dee's new beau playing Oliver to Nick's Fagin. She's told me that he is catty and rude to her when she is over at the band's rehearsals, making snide comments about her supposedly uptight demeanor and far too L7 public image for a wild man that fronts a punk band. The guy's a haunt. This naturally sets me off into kamikaze mode--for all my pontificating about leaving the boy I was back in Wellesley, cruelty to my friends, especially the women gets me into a fighting state of mind. And I have no doubt that I could stomp the living crap out of that emaciated old creep--say the word.

And I am crazy about Dee, which doesn't help.

The gig's a good one already, Saturday night at the Rat and some of my favorite people are already through the door. The beautiful and doe eyed Judy Stripes and her hyperactive sister Lo, they never stop shimmying up front on a good second set, Crazy Rachel, David's prior girl with her best pal, Jeri-Anne, a soft spoken sweetheart, the Squids, a bunch of Navy dudes from a local base that have us doing "the Gator", an on the filthy floor epileptic rug cut among the spit and sweat and all our regulars--our friends finish their rama-lama drop the hammer opening, now it's our turn. Best of all, I see a small group of people that I recognize as creme de la jock creme from my freaking high school class--word's gotten out, they tell me, that I have become this crazed weirdo freak and they wanna see if the emmis is in fact the emmis.

I won't let them down. But I don't want too many of MY current people seeing ME talk to those rod-asses from Wellesley (in their fucking penny loafers at the Rat?). The tables haven't just turned, the whole banquet hall is now upside down, social strata wise. High school is OVER!

We saunter out and turn up the volume and tempo accordingly and that sort of pins the not quite inebriated folks back to the walls, except a few hardy souls like our friend Little Stevie. He shakes and trembles in time to the thrash as if wired or hopping on a hot plate in front of me and it's all good, but what the flying fuck is happening here? My Wellesley classmates surround him and start shoving him back and forth like he's a black clad hot-plate and the other dancers scatter, fearing they'll get hurt, too. I'm about to hop off the stage to protect him from these upper crust vermin when the almighty wrath of the Rat staff sets upon them like a phalanx of Special Forces-- Eddie, Doug, Rick, Eric—and they do not collar Stevie for the haul-away as you'd figure they'd side with the jocks, they are jocks themselves. They don't. Nope, we punks are their bread and butter, we're like peacocks in the palace of kings and so my former peers are hustled out the back and given the "dumpster job" par thorough. All of them tossed in that rodent infested metal bin like yesterday's refuse, bloodied and as pulped as their morning OJ was when served to them by daddy's domestic. They're rat-meat if they don't wake up fast enough or if they do, just plain flotsam and jetsam way out of their element and if I may quote one of our tunes, "don't come back".

Set ends and we're packed in the dressing room together at the far end of the club. Barb and Mike and I changing our clothes, Merle schmoozing with some out of towners and our buddies in the other group tuning up and Dee is snuggling with David and what can you do? Rowland, that sack of weasel droppings is nattering away about a next set and glaring with red eyed fury at Dee. I see it and say nothing--ain't my fight, ain't my war. In a move of exaggerated politesse, he hands her a fresh cold Bud and bows like the lame assed non-thespian he is. And flutters out the door.

David is shaking his head at this farcical charade and leans over to ask me if we're doing our song "When Ya Gonna Quit" in our next set. It is a mean spirited and IMHO totally accurate ode to the parasite lounging in the "dressing room". The only thing it doesn't have is Barb singing it in a lisp. Needless to say David loves it--but will have to wait for the end of his own set which is pending, for us to set up and bang it out.

Off they go to the stage with Dee and a few other friends in a small pack behind them. Me, I take up residence at the bar and start gumming back and forth with blond Jimmy, my favorite tender there and also a Wellesley guy. When I tell him about the beating our former neighbors got, he just shakes his head--you don't know the customs, don't fuck with the natives.

David's crew starts pumping out their sweet and speedy songs one after the other without stopping as we do, as do most of the other bands. Why waste time, why banter, when all you want is that momentum, that headlong rush where the body is present and the brain disappears. And the dance floor fills up and the night is headed for that nirvana that Saturdays promise to be and rarely deliver.

About halfway in, though, you can feel and see the mood in the pogo pit change and the band is clearly distracted. Someone is getting pushed back and forth, shit, why is it that some people cannot hold their booze enough to at least pass out before they make asses of themselves, I wonder which suburban nitwit overdid it and is headed to join the Wellesley losers in the back of the venue. I am endlessly curious and wander over to see who this night's "pass-around fuckup" is.

And my heart nearly stops and my face freezes. It's Dee.

Her eyes rolling in her head, more white than pupils, she is lurching from couple to couple, hanging onto their necks the rails of a sinking ocean liner. They shove her away and into the mucky grime of the dance floor and I elbow aside enough of them to pick her up. Her eyes slot-machine for a second until they focus on mine as I try to haul her out of there.

"Hey, Johnny, what's goin' on, baby, wooo," she blathers out. This isn't booze--she barely drinks as is. The rubber legs, shit, last time I saw this was back in HS when it was "714 Day"--the quaaludes came in in the morning, the ambulances took the kids away in the afternoon. But this is way past Sopors. I don't know what's in her veins, but her equilibrium has just boarded a plane to Timbuktu.

"Dee, what the hell did you do?"

"I din't do nuthin', Johnny", she replied, head moving side to side like the needle on a VU meter. Then, out of nowhere, she perked up and said "hey, I wanna sing, I can sing better n Barb, you know that, right?"

"Sure, Dee, sure". And I was thinking how I gotta get her out of there, but she wriggled free and vaulted, all knock kneed and wild eyed onto the stage and snatched the mic from her date!

"Ummgmmfmmdmmm" or something like it as the band stopped and she fell right over the monitors, but still clinging to the mic stand as Dave picked her up.

"Hey, babe, wooo, can I fuckin' sing, man, right?"

The bouncers at this point assemble at the side of the stage--a drunken BC football lout of suburban preppie twit type was no problem, a petite female was. They decided to let us handle it for the moment and when Dave tried to gently pry her loose, she lit into him.

"Hey, I can sing if I wanna, fush you man, let me sing". As he tried to firmly pull the mic from her and move her to the side of the stage, she dug in--whatever she was dosed with appeared to give the cute little nursing student from Upstate NY a ton of strength.

"I'm gonna sing, man.....hey, c'mon play something, I wanna sing". And then she pulled the mic stand away and glared at him and said "you're no fun, no fun, I wanna see my Johnny up here, where's Johnny"?

Oh no. Oh no no no.

"Where's my Johnny? Oh Johnnnneeeee—get up here, come on, show 'em what you got, oh, he has such a cock….hahahaha"…

I would like to crawl into a hole and die. Before she could launch into an even more concise if blithered treatise on my organ (which was surely coming next, the exegesis, not me), she fell over to her side, dropping the mic. The bouncing crew picked her up and proceeded to try and carry her up the back stairs.

I met them at the bottom of the stairway. "Let me handle this, I'll get her a cab, just don't hurt her, she's really fucked up, man".

They dropped her onto the fetid, stinking carpet, one of them, I don't know which said "she's all yours, big dick" and they laughed, leaving her in a heap. I picked her up and threw her over my shoulder and turned to take her upstairs when I stood face to face with Nick Rowland.

"What a sleazy little lowlife she is—my goodness, she really doesn't belong here". And leered at me to let me know what exactly had gone down, but with Dee on my back and a set to play in twenty minutes all I had time for was to get up the back stairs, around the bank to the cab stand and get her home--I opened the back of a black and white Town Taxi set her in it and said "Beth Israel ER-- now". Handed the hack a tenner and headed back to the club.

No Saturday night nirvana. Audience in shock. My friend's no longer speaking to me, one does not mess with a peer's woman, or more accurately, get caught doing it. Let it be 2AM as soon as possible and let this nightmare end.

....
....
....

As the sun slowly rose pink and orange through the Atlantic's mist over the city on Sunday, the detritus of the college town party--the empties, the piss-stained sidewalks, half eaten burger and fries combos--is lit up like the morning after a minor battle. Eerily quiet before the older folks shuffle into St Whatever's pews for absolution, the Sunday Globe and Herald delivered, a sweet cup or two of coffee for the first shifters everywhere-- it's strangely somber, like the only break the city really gets, these precious hours.

Laid out on a gurney in the ER is another version of same, stomach pumped and slumbering, Dee McClain. By noon she'll be released, vertical, bleary eyed and completely ashamed of something not her fault, something she deserved no blame in, but something that she knew would mark her forever in that back stabbing gossipy seaport. Time to start over and immediately, where the people are forgiving and she can sink in anonymous and fresh and her sins washed away from her like the tangible wreckage of last night into the gutters of memory.

By nine PM, her little car is packed with all she needs, Mom and dad will send a truck for the furniture. She's headed for shelter and safety.

In New York City. New York Fucking City.

Chapter 8, Cyberspace/Facebook/September 2013.

JOHNNYANGELWENDELL: Hey, Blondie!

VIVDeMILO: LOL, yeah right. You like my new photo?

JOHNNYANGELWENDELL: Once I hadda luv and it was a gas/soon turned out/Viv's a pain in the ass

VIVDeMILO: LOL...on a roll today are we?

JOHNNYANGELWENDELL: I am liking that picture of you. You took it?

VIVDeMILO: Yes.

JOHNNYANGELWENDELL: What's news, what's happening?

VIVDeMILO: With me or with Dee?

JOHNNYANGELWENDELL: Both, either, all points in between.

VIVDeMILO: Waiting on a few fashion shoots, talking to the city about shooting special events, et cetera.

JOHNNYANGELWENDELL: Fashion shoots in North Florida? What's the couture--gator hide and burlap?

VIVDeMILO: LOL. Oh, it isn't completely backwards here. Well, maybe a bit.

JOHNNYANGELWENDELL: You a Boston girl, lived in SF and here in LA, that shit must make you 5150?

VIVDeMILO: Pardon?

VIVDeMILO: 5150?

JOHNNYANGELWENDELL: Crazy. LAPD expression thing.

VIVDeMILO: Oh. Well, yes--I loved the Bay Area but now I don't even think I could afford to be homeless there. So, here I stay.

JOHNNYANGELWENDELL: Shooting Ellie Mae Clampett beauty pageants and steroid swollen Jethro's greased up and grimacing with their tiny balls flopping in their Speedos.

VIVDeMILO: LOL. You do have a way with words. That's what Dee loved about you or one of the things she did.

JOHNNYANGELWENDELL: I'm a little surprised to hear the expression "Dee loved about you", Viv. I think she was amused by me and we had a good time together, but love?

VIVDeMILO: You never knew?

JOHNNYANGELWENDELL: Knew what? Dee was with all of my friends, I was just another bad boy guy she notched on her pubic belt, you know?

VIVDeMILO: Oh no. Not at all. Oh wow--you had no idea.
JOHNNYANGELWENDELL: This is fucking my shit up bad, Viv--what are you talking about?
VIVDeMILO: Dee loved you.
JOHNNYANGELWENDELL: No way. No way at all. She ever tell you that? Or is that one of those off in the distance perceptions of yours?
VIVDeMILO: She thought the others were fun guys and all but you were the one that really stole her heart. She told me that one day the two of you would be together.
JOHNNYANGELWENDELL: I never had any inkling of that. Why didn't she ever say anything?
VIVDeMILO: I think she was waiting for you. You are a man, you know.
JOHNNYANGELWENDELL: Last I checked, let me look. Yeah, still a man.
JOHNNYANGELWENDELL: That isn't my style, it's never been. I don't make those moves, you can get hurt.
VIVDeMILO: Then I guess you two had more in common with each other than you realized, yes?
JOHNNYANGEL: Touche. Point to the yellow head vixen.
VIVDeMILO: LOL
VIVDeMILO: I found her brother online. I sent him a few emails. Nothing. Google turns up nothing, either.
JOHNNYANGELWENDELL: Hmm.

JOHNNYANGELWENDELL: You still have connections at any of your old magazines, the ones you free-lanced for?

VIVDeMILO: Yes, why?

JOHNNYANGELWENDELL: Call a few of the reporters and ask them to look up "McClain, New York" in a Lexis/Nexis database--that's what all the PI's use, it's the shit. That may get you death records, criminal, something.

VIVDeMILO: OK. Lexis/Nexis. Got it.

JOHNNYANGELWENDELL: You'll find her one way or another.....heeheehee.

VIVDeMILO: LOL. It never stops.

JOHNNYANGELWENDELL: No, it doesn't. But you gotta tell me, why the fuck did Dee split town if I was really the one she wanted?

VIVDeMILO: Maybe she didn't think she could face you after that scene, I have no idea. If we find her, we'll ask, if she remembers or wants to talk about it.

VIVDeMILO: I have to run, my darling.

JOHNNYANGELWENDELL: Ooh, my darling, I like that. Maybe you can, wait for it, here it comes...CALL ME! Oh, the rapture!

VIVDeMILO: LOL. On that sour note, ciao, J.

JOHNNYANGELWENDELL: See ya, V.

Chapter 9/Viv's tale/Florida/2013.

Viv DeMilo reckoned that the reason she loved punk rock so much when she first discovered and heard it was because it was the first thing monolithic and loud enough to drive her parent's cruel asides out of her head. "Are you ever going to amount to anything at all" from her harsh, ax-faced old man or the contempt-laden tut-tut's of her mother were number one on her internal hit/shit parade endlessly replaying in the jukebox that was her brain.

She also reckoned, after many years of therapy, meditation and decent Humboldt herb, that her natural stance of distance and carefully contrived persona of introspection were a reaction to their unceasing meanness. Not wanting to be hurt but refusing to retreat meant a middle ground she'd always occupied. That of the negotiator and the good buddy whose shoulder was always for rent. It did bug her from time to time that no one ever seemed to offer the same to her but after all the ups and downs of a career photographer, at this point, she was happy to be still drawing breath from outside her most dreaded fear, a cubicle.

It was as a bemused observer of human perfidy that she first noticed the woman that would become her best friend for a time, Miss Dee McClain. Viv at that moment was Linda Boudreaux, a South Shore girl with a pleasant if anonymous smile and brownish straight hair, someone you wouldn't notice unless she maybe spilled scalding coffee on you at Dunky's. One of her friends was chummy with a group of brothers that had a pleasant if innocuous power pop group and suggested they journey into Boston to see them at this exotic punk club, Cantone's. To Viv at the time, it may as well have been the Museum of Science as her interest in music--even the Beatles-ish warble of her neighbors--was inconsequential. She wanted to be an artist.

Venture she did and after her friend's combo was done and off the area designated as "stage", another group set up, a loud, frenetic punk band with a hyperactive, red-headed, knock-kneed pretty boy singer. This in and of itself would have gotten her attention (strictly from the standpoint of art, you see), but even more striking was the beautiful blond woman that fixed herself directly in front of him, feet planted defiantly in a stance that screamed "stand by your man" more defiantly that a battalion of Tammy Wynette's. Staking out her "lead singer's chick" turf as plainly and clearly as day was her soon to be BFF, Ms. Dee McClain.

Between the jackhammer slam-a-rama of the band and her fascination with the almost blood thick loyalty of the blond girl in front, Viv had her Saul to Damascus moment. Amid the rancid stink of cheap beer and stale marinara (the joint was in fact an Italian restaurant by day), she was converted. And in a rare moment of aggression, she got up next to the blond girl and started hopping madly herself to the beat of this powerful, primal pounding.

After a few numbers, the band paused to collect itself and Dee decided to size up this intruder, friend or foe.

"I'm Dee--who are you?"

"I'm Linda", Viv said, her voice trailing off as it tended to and Dee made her repeat her name a few times until she got it.

"You ever seen them before?" asked Dee, gesturing to the band.

"No. They're really good, I mean, I've never heard anything like this before". Was true. In reality, other than her older sister's collections of hippie classics, there wasn't much she'd ever really sampled.

"Well, you should come down here every night then," said Dee. "There's so many great bands, the Real Kids, Unnatural Axe, LaPeste, the Nervous Eaters, Thrills--it's great, I never knew anything like this when I was in high school in Rawchester" (Rochester, NY--Dee's upstate drawl always elongated itself on that word with hometown pride and revulsion).

"Maybe I will.....hey, call me when they're playing again", said Viv/Linda, pointing to the band. Dee motioned to Linda/Viv to get a pen out of purse and a piece of paper and when Dee put the note down to exchange numbers, a swaying boozehound of the overweight townie variety in a leather jacket and flopping stained black jeans crashed into her, spilling her beer on the table and note.

"Hey, fat-ass, watch what the fuck you're doing," she declaimed loudly in the pudgy punker's face. Linda/Viv was absolutely astonished--she had never heard a woman--certainly not a petite little suburban kitten like this one sass some local hoodlum. The chunky barfly raised his hands as if to say he was sorry, and Linda/Viv was impressed--this Dee was all right.

A few days later, Dee rang L/V up at her parent's house and ran down what was her drill for the coming Saturday--rise at noon, scour a few record shops and tune into the one punk rock radio show on, "The Demi Monde", hosted by a serious sounding fellow named Oedipus. Linda dutifully tuned her car radio to 88.1 WTBS at the proscribed time and on came a slew of songs that did to Ms. Boudreaux exactly what was described so perfectly by Lou Reed's Janey--she couldn't believe what she'd heard at all. Especially one song, the scraping fracture of "Venus De Milo" by New York's Television. From that moment on, Linda was dead, and Vivienne DeMilo (Linda was too self-conscious to ever be a complete copycat) was born.

She plunged soul deep into the actual demimonde of Boston's underground scene, bringing her camera everywhere and the flared corduroys and drab brown shoes of her past were replaced by mini-skirts and heels and the dull blue hues of her neat jean tops gave way to tight blouses of more spectacular shade. Strangely enough, this display of satori bravado was not in awe of Dee, who still dressed semi-conservatively--Viv sussed that her friend wasn't as parent free as she'd led on to be. Fact was, Dee was a total dependent, minus their allowances for rent and food and "amenities", Dee was a broke assed college girl.

Which meant her rebellion was subtle. But Viv could sense it was acute in its way, the boys Dee liked were all kind of rough looking, but all generally good natured and kind hearted and not thuggish at all, with one exception, the tart-tongued and attitudinal guitar player in Thrills, Johnny Angel. He was a brusque, rude, curt little jerk in Viv's estimation and even worse, indifferent to her heroine's adoration. Dee tended to love 'em and leave 'em with a gusto, but that prick actually slept with her once and never brought it up again like it was meaningless sex. In Viv's eyes, living her life out vicariously through the great blond liberator of Rochester, well, that was an absolute toss down of the gauntlet. How dare he?

Which is why, 35 years later, she was so amazed to find herself in conversation with him on a regular basis, albeit across a continent. She was certain that he--the only man she thought that walked away from Dee McClain unscarred--would have some knowledge of her whereabouts or at least not take serious offense to being asked to join the search. She was also amazed to find that his foul-mouthed punk rock persona of the Carter era was just as much of a put on as Dee's was or for that matter, her own. He was generally a middle aged, exercise-junkie dad doting on his sons or talking politics. He took a keen interest in what she did, offered startling critiques of Viv's photos and boosted her spirits every time they chatted.

As per his suggestion, she called up an old colleague of hers in Oakland, an investigative reporter with the East Bay Express. After exchanging a few tidbits of catch up, she asked what Johnny had suggested and in fact, her old friend in Bay Area did have that expensive search engine on his home rig.

"Viv, let me get back to you in a few, K" he said and she said she appreciated it with the slight hint of seductive lilt in her reply--one thing she'd definitely learned from Dee was that men could be charmed so easily, why not do it if it got you what you wanted.

After she hung up, she laughed to herself. The only man Dee's charms bounced off of, that one-time sullen squirt Johnny Angel--was now her ally in the great search to find her. And it seems that even he was moved a bit by Dee more than he ever let on back when that kind of thing moved mountains in a 20-something's head. The more she learned, the less she was sure of--other than if I don't get back to 2013, I don't eat this week. Dee can wait. Life isn't going to.

Chapter 10/Somewhere near Hartford Ct/ May, 1979.

"Mikey, pull the fuck over and get off this fucking highway, man--we're out of beer!"

One hundred miles outside of Boston and already dry. Why the band booze-a-thon? Well, we are celebrating, unsuspecting world, we are on the way the up the ladder to....well, somewhere, I'm half faced as is. Three quarters faced to be excruciatingly accurate and you know me, a stickler for numerical perfection.

Oh, screw the prose--where are we headed? To Mecca, mofo--we are on our first trip to play New York City, a relatively new joint called Hurrah, uptown near Lincoln Center and we Thrills are thrilled to the gills. Hammered too, because we're all a little nervous. This is not no laughing matter here--allegedly and purportedly, we're being looked at by various bigwigs. Barb is handling this end of the deal--her day job for a while was at the big rock FM in Boston and those powerhouses have set up this show, supporting a British band also fronted by a woman, Penetration. Merle and I are enormous fans of this band and so naturally we're putting the brews to rest at what I reckon is one killed every twenty miles. We need more and quick. And a piss stop. My bladder feels like someone's stuffed the Goodyear Blimp under my navel.

It has to be said that the enormity of a first gig in New York is not a trifling thing to a Boston band. Or any significant event where a Bostonian has become a peer to a New Yorker in any way. We are raised to seethe on the issue of our inferiority to the juggernaut to the southwest despite our town being settled first. Of course it's a one-sided rivalry--like Philly is to NYC or anywhere else, being a satellite city, we care what they think and they don't care about us. So, that little bit of nonsense has sent the hops craving into the ozone.

Mike, drummer and driver, is not drinking. Such a responsible fellow. More accurately, he has already realized that uncaged from our normal zoo, his band-mates are probably better a few sheets to the wind, otherwise we'd be ricocheting off the walls of the van with nervous energy, wrassling, yipping and screaming and the last thing he wants is to be Eddie Cochran'ed at 21 years old on the I-95.

Eagle eyed whilst pie-eyed I am and I spot the bright lights of a mall off on a rise in some town called Weathersfield. Mike steers the band kayak into the lot, dippy Johnny hops out while the van is still moving and nearly head butts an embankment but I don't care because I'm on the road and this is fan-fucking-tastic. Quite a change in attitude from the day before when I called Barb yowling about how I ain't going anywhere. Talked off that absurd ledge, here I be and dousing the flames of edge and nerves with Budweiser talls--it was one loony tunes couple of weeks leading to this and the roof is torn off the Johnny sucker this evening.

You see, my dearly beloved, a couple of weeks ago, we'd done a gig in Cambridge at Inn Square Men's Bar, a place where we didn't really do too well as a rule. (As was always the case in Cambridge, cross the mighty Charles and the many headed hydra of hippie was still alive and well and Summer of Love types we weren't.) This gig was decent enough but as Cambridge was last call at 1AM and Boston's on the deuce, over the river to Grandma's Rat we go to close out the evening.

On the way out of Kenmore Square to stumble over the little bridge that arced over the Pike to my studio, I ran into this rather tall, exotic looking blond lady that I vaguely recognized as a Thrills gig regular. She was a big, pale girl, towering over me and very friendly with a Midwestern twang and Betty Boop curls and as one thing led to another by way of very sparse conversation, t'was off to her palace in faraway Jamaica Plain, where we proceeded to sloppily slobber all over each other and subsequently bang away like a caboose shambling down at the end of a long train.

It may have been an hour after post-cum doze that I awoke to the sensation of having my noggin smashed in. What my brand new friend had foolishly omitted from our intense pre-copulation conference was that she had a live in boyfriend, one considerably bigger than her, which meant a man mountain twice my size, raining blows on my pretty little head like Thor's hammer.

Quickly regaining what little sense I had, I grabbed my jeans and slid away from this brutal beating into the loo, where I locked the door right quick and tried to figure out how to escape from this bedlam in one piece. Hulk man is banging on the door screaming how he's gonna kill that fucking Johnny Angel, oh the horrible flip-side of celebrity! I can hear her and she's pleading clemency for me and maybe her too. The instinct to live sends one's IQ up about 50 points when it's doused with adrenalin and I gauged the second floor window of the bathroom just large enough to jump out of and not get too badly hurt--out I went, but lucky as lucky gets, the fire escape was only a small swing out on the ledge and down I went to Center Street intact. All the way out the window I could hear the boozy Bickerson's battling, her wailing and his cursing. It had not yet dawned on me that barefoot and only in jeans, my jacket and shirt and shoes were still in their flat and going back there was not a serious possibility if I wanted to retain my teeth at the very least. I wasn't gonna die of exposure or cold or anything but a carload of Townies returning from a disco without the soothing salve of women would certainly to love to get their rocks off beating some lone and lost whacko trying to find his way home. They did this to punks with all their clothes on in Kenmore Square all the time.

As if by the hand of the punk rock god drawn to the road by my "Iggy on the cover of "Raw Power" outfit, Boston's finest pulled up. No neighbor had called the cops, they were just plain there in the Plain. I waved them over and explained my sad plight and so up they went to the House of the Rising Fist and collected my goods for me. Both of them came back down laughing their beefy Irish asses off.

"What the hell were you thinking, son?" asked one of them and I shrugged. The other, a kindly white maned old fellow probably about to retire looked me straight in my bleary eyes and asked a question that had probably been brewing in his cerebellum since getting a look at my Gulliver like assailant.

"Well, kid--was she worth it?"

I had no answer for that. I did ask for a ride back to the Fens and they politely declined. Not on their beat. As my head cleared, I realized that the beast that battered me played in Mackie's new band, who rehearsed in our space. Putting two and two together, I sauntered over to a payphone and read the poor fellow Mr. Mack (Merle's roomie at this point) the riot act--come down here and get me or your band's gear's in the street tomorrow.

Which he did and a few days later, his guitar player and I agreed to a truce--I had no idea who she was and apparently this happened with embarrassing frequency which made both of us feel like crap. Unfortunately, whatever I did in my brief turn with her lit up her life like Debbie Boone, man (told you it was temporary)--she began turning up at my door at 3AM absolutely wasted and demanding to be cleaved and as I am really helpless when an invitingly drenched pussy is waved at me, I obliged. Until the day before this trip--I put my sleepy little foot down and said no more when she came up to the crash pad. But the damage had been done--I hadn't really slept a night in two weeks.

....
...

So, I am now seven-eighths crazy and hammered when we cross from Westchester into the Bronx. The plan is to drop all our gear off at Arturo Vega's loft on Bowery--he offered his place for equipment and to zonk out there, his former tenants and charges, Dee Dee and Joey Ramone now had places of their own. Because none of us had talked to Arty in about a week, he'd forgotten so when we arrive at the place, naturally, no one's home, We're right and well screwed, but somehow in my stupor, I remember I have good ole Charlie Roth's number up on 10th and so we luckily we can drop the stuff off and disperse. Everyone has a place to go, yes?

Not me. I got nothing to do and nowhere to go, I already AM sedated, you see. Fumbling through the same pockets that had produced Charlie's phone also got me Donna's, a lovely woman that was best friends with a woman whose partner was my best friend from high school. She was pleased to hear from me--how fortunate and what are you doing and meet me at the Mudd Club, I wanna go!

Charlie was laughing at our pitiful lack of road decorum when we alighted at 85 E10th. He's a veteran and we're novices and luckily he's also kind. Saved.

Beats me how I got to the Mudd, I think I told Mike that's where I was sleeping and got dumped in the no-man's land where that little ole bar was located , so this is where I end up, sweet. Donna arrives shortly afterwards by cab and either she has some kind of juice or I look appropriately colorful, we sleaze and ease right to the front of the line and into the room--so this is where it's at now, right?

Man this place is just too fucking amazing and damn--Oedipus is here, down from Boston to cheer us on and hang with all the hotshots and hot shits that were now doing the buddy-buddy suck-up up rhumba to him, as he's now running that big FM all the way up the dial. The same FM has been playing the absolute shit out of our first single and I'm gonna get one to the DJ. Donna looks at me cross-eyed and askance as that is a serious protocol breach and do I care? Of course I don't. I hand it to him and ten minutes later "I'll Be the Heartbreaker" is getting the bodies moving. I'm getting played in New York!

More importantly, am I getting laid in New York? All the bands that come up the road to share bills with us at the Rat and Cantone's are men and I haven't been here in two years. The prerogative of the rocker on road is the mindless encounter and right now, my mind is gone, so I'm at least halfway right. And Donna seems to have disappeared in the Byzantine layout of this muddy Mudd. So, antsy as hell I am getting when I am face to face again with my one time hero, Mister David Johansen, former singer, New York Dolls.

Did I tell you that I never forget a slight and that David--my idol, front man of the greatest band that ever existed--took a swing at me last year? I guess I forgot to tell you about that one. DJ had played a show at the Orpheum in between the Ramones and Willie Loco and was guzzling whisky afterwards at the Rat himself when I literally ran into him on the way out of the can. I smiled at him and said "great set, man--I loved it".

And he socked me.

I was more hurt than hurt if you know what I mean (the man's got to be what, 130 pounds soaking wet) and I got totally wasted past my normal madness and after this humiliation bedded a woman that claimed I was her first male ever later (I'm not bragging here, it did freak me out a little to be told that my muff-chomping skills were on a par with her typical shack ups. Baby, I was born to lezz). So, face to face with Johansen again, my dander and BP are soaring man, time to give YOU a personality crisis starting with your teeth.

Oedipus sees this and hauls my ass into a corner for "Wake The Fuck Up 101". "This is New York,

Johnny, you cannot hit David Johansen, half the people here will be bragging tomorrow that they killed some drunk crazy that slapped him around, drop it, OK?"

Of course he's right. And Donna chides me all the way out the door and into taxi to her place uptown where she informs me that the candy store is closed. She still lives in this tiny apartment with her ex-boyfriend. What in tarnation? No sex? We huggle and snuggle and all as he snores away on the couch but the genitalia don't touch so it ain't all that much. How they do it without homicide is beyond me, but in the morning, he heads out to work and she rises leisurely with me, now both sober (excruciatingly hungover in my case) and not particularly wanting to be in each other's company--she's a pretty woman and a very kind one to boot, but when the mouth is cotton and there's a Sahara of sand running in my veins, generally I have ceased amorousness a while back. She assures me she will see me at Hurrah later.

Well, it is six hours to sound-check and I'm on the isle of Manhattan all by my lonesome and so I do what I always do when traveling, I ramble. Doesn't matter where it is, I can't sit still and so I take the subway to Cooper Union because I remember Charlie's down near there, but I take the wrong turn and end up on St. Marks Place completely by chance and run into a huge crew of Thrills kids down to support us--like stepping through the looking glass or like when "The Wizard Of Oz" goes all color, I can forget my throbbing skull and sore nuts for at least a bit.

Most of 8th Street's haberdashers play in bands and all of them have been north, so I can hang easy with them, my boys the Rousers who have promised we'll play Max's with them next time down, Jimi and Rich from the Dots, Tish and Snooky over at Manic Panic--this is like Mecca, every weirdo from the tri-state area and beyond has remade themselves into this off-kilter tribe of happy to spit in yer eye sir freakazoid madness. And yeah, we'll all come uptown to see you, Mr J--guest list, por favor?

Of course--so glad to be of service and at your service!

Hurrah, as it turns out, appears to be a former loft turned live music space and the stage is jammed way back in the corner so at sound-check, we are blaring out like from a giant speaker and it is seriously crummy sounding onstage. Our sound-man is Granny, Barb's dour, jaded boyfriend who regales us of tales of brave Aerosmith tours when he tekked for them. He is doing the best he can but even he cannot work miracles and I am starting to feel the cold clammy hand of bombing in New York creepy crawling up my spine.

Granny does reassure us that when bodies enter the loft, they'll absorb the sound and we'll be groovy plus. Gamely we ascend the steps and peer out into total darkness and Mike kicks in "Wait For Me"s big beat and the train starts a rolling and through our numbers we blast, never stopping, never giving anyone a chance to wander off, upping the tempo until we get to our big crescendo, "Hey! (Not Another Face In The Crowd")

Every punk band--oh shit, everybody's--got a theme song, one tune they're identified with. And this one is ours, a simple chant of "hey, come n lookamee baby cos I'm not another face in da crowd" 16 times over two and a half minutes with a few verses a terrible solo from me and a coda, quite similar in feel and construction to the Dolls' "Trash" but frenzied and really rockabilly lilting, which is pretty much the strangest thing about our band. Despite all the permutations of punk, half our material swings and sways like the Grand Ole Opry on benzadrine. "Hey" is the most extreme example, slowed down, it would be all cowpoke, but probably only I hear it that way. Took me three minutes tops to write it, first time it was played out, fists went in the air on the "hey" and for the first time in my existence, I felt like I actually moved the psychic needle of life just a tad.

Our people from Boston did just that, the "hey" fist pump on the last tune and done we were. Not too terrible at all, I feel all right, we didn't die and I get an attaboy nod from Talking Heads singer David Byrne as I strut to the dressing room, where Penetration has decided they don't want us penetrating their space and pull rank and we're 86ed-- uppity tea bag wankers, oh the indignity. What is with the exports from the UK anyway? Last year, we gigged with the Stranglers at the Rat and those arrogant cretins made us set up in front of them--at the friggin' Rat? The bouncers had to build a stage extension or we'd be on the dance floor getting our toes trod upon. And not too long ago, this har har waste of British oxygen called "the Fabulous Poodles"--they headlined and we drew everyone. So, their hoity-toity managers informed us that the second set was to be 20 minutes long and no two encores.

The only thing worse than the English are the Anglophiles that enable this acceptable rudeness. I see kids in Union Jacks at gigs and I get hives.

Well, what to do now? To the bar, Splivins, the bar and more beer for the visiting dignitary and a bit of schmooze with the head of IRS (label, not tax agency) who says we're pretty good but they're really into signing this new band, the Cramps (new my ass, I'd seen them years ago and shared pizza with them after they were booed off the Rat's stage. They were killer fantastic and I told them that they'd be welcomed lovingly every time they returned and so far that had been true).

Swiveling away from the exec fella, I see a gaggle of people just up the stairs in the middle of the bar with a bunch of black clad grebos, all surrounding one blond head. Upon further examination, holy shit, it's Blondie--Debbie Harry herself and Chris and Nigel and Frank. I have to meet her, I just gotta--not because I fancy her (or think I'd ever have a chance with the almighty reina de newavo wavo), but because I wanna pay props. So, I race into the dressing room (fuck the limeys, let them shoot up in the bathroom like proper musicians), grab a "Heartbreaker/Hey" single and ease on over to her majesty.

"Uhm, hey, we just played here and this is my single and I hope you like it and congratulations on "Heart of Glass" going to number one and is there gonna be a disco song on the next record too?" All in one breath. I should have been a sax player.

She smiled and took the 45 and told me they were working on a disco song and thanks. Oh man, this night is so amazing it can't possibly get any better.

But it did.

From out of the darkness of the corner of the room, I saw someone waving at me and this eerie old feeling from the back of my mind started singing its song to me, damn, there she was. Dee McClain. Dee--I hadn't seen her in a year but the blazing eyes and that huge smile, she skipped over to me and with a "Johnnneee" threw her arms around my neck and gave me a great big kiss, muah!

I was so glad to see her but that vibe--the vibe you get when you quickly remember your role in someone's life--made me kind of freeze just a little. That and she was different. Her blond hair was jet black and she was even more rail like skinny that I recalled. And in leather and pegged black jeans like a punk rock girl.

We catch up quick. She'd been living in a flat downstairs from her parents on Murray Hill but that didn't work out and she got her own place in Chelsea. She was between jobs and not in school. And I was free of the horrible harridan of Marlborough Street and let's have a drink or two and keep talking, maybe?

She sets me off like no one else though, damn it. Even after this transformation from cute little sweetheart to noir semi-urchin, she's goddamned fucking Dee, the one I want more than anyone else, the one that slides through my mitts like lubed eels, the elusive prize and yet, I can't ever let on because maybe somewhere in my mind I know that by being the one web-free fly, Spider McClain will always stay near me. If she can't have me, she'll want me that much more. Maze-like logic, but I trust this instinct--because to not do so would be fatal, I think.

I suggest we take a walk or something, just get away from my band-mates and our contingent of New England admirers, all of who are presently furious with me for not sharing my new friend Debbie Harry's time with them. Chickenshits, go bug her yourselves, I think, but arm in arm with Dee, we stride down 64th as a mist is dropping on the city and then we stop and face each other as if on the same beat and start sucking each other's lips, me wanting to just tear her apart right there on the street and she seemingly of the same mind.

We turn to go back to Hurrah, but Dee stops me before we go back up the stairs. Let's go to Max's, she suggests, she's a regular there, it's free, I can meet all her new friends and I am pondering this as we sit on a cold stone step near where the band van is parked.

We embrace and kiss again, just gorging ourselves on each other, like as if to swallow each other's faces. She pulls her face away for a moment and smiles that satanic little grin of hers and tells me there's an important matter we must discuss.

"I've been thinking that I really need to do this one thing", she says and as I tip my head inquisitively, she drops her hand onto my lap and begins to run her palm up and down along the increasingly prominent bulge in my jeans.

"You did me and I have to do you".

And deftly and with no resistance from me, she undoes my jeans and pulls my cock out, right there in the alley and smiles and drops diver like on it. At first, gently circling my swollen aching cock's head with that pink perfection of a tongue, she gradually eases lower and lower until I am fully inside her mouth, her head moving piston like faster and faster, her tongue dancing on the underside of my cock like a spongy ballerina. My actual brain, the one in my proper head is also going into overdrive--not quite so over-driven that I can't hear the familiar voices of my band-mates and sound-man on the other side of the van. As they turn the corner, all of them get a fair viewing of the hastily terminated blow job and all try not to crack up at the sight of fearless leader getting head on a New York City street. Button up, buttercup and make those jeans snap snappy.

"Uh, guys, I think I'm gonna go to Max's with Dee, you remember Dee, used to live in Boston, right?" Uncomfortable acknowledgement. And then the stern lecture from Barb--we have a gig tomorrow in Boston or did you forget?

"No, I know", I say, rising to stand and helping Dee off her perch. "I'll take the train up tomorrow and meet you there. I wanna hang with Dee here in the city".

"No fucking way, Johnny", says Barb. In many ways, she's way closer to me than any other woman and knows that once I leave with this crow-headed usurper, I'll stay in Manhattan (and in Dee) for three days, gigs be damned.
"Come on, Johnny, let's go", implores Mike, who is actually going to work the next day on no sleep after a four hour drive. And I'm the nutty one here?

And I'm hustled into the van with gig bag tossed in after me by Granny. Dee makes a little wave at me, turns on her heel and disappears into the night, no kiss goodbye, just a taxi hailed to 17th Street and Max's and gone like a cool breeze.

Me, I had like a dozen free brews at the Hurrah bar and with no love object in hand or lap, out I go. I don't open my eyes again until Framingham. The maiden voyage to the city is complete. Over and (passed) out.

Chapter 11/Boston/June, 1979.

A year and a half into the life of Thrills and it's become clear that what was a bash and crash chaos fest at its birth is now a viable rock band. And I have to admit, this is making us all a little crazier than we already were at formation and why wouldn't it? Almost all of our goofy and spoofy joke punk numbers have been retired and the "high speed anthems of love's hurt" are 90% of our set. So much so that when the twin topical goldmines of recent times---the meltdown at Three Mile Island and the story of Brenda Spencer the San Diego sniper crossed my hyperactive cortex, they inspired two new songs. The former a parody of "There's Gonna Be A Showdown" with "meltdown" replacing the Archie Bell/Dolls original replete with couplets about glowing mutants and the like and the latter a cheery recitation of the events of the SoCal massacre simply entitled "Brenda Spencer". Both nixed by the band as already dated by our newly minted standard as Serious Band. The latter is now called "The Last to Know", another love-dove disappointment warble. Because that topic could never be a Top 40 success, right?

We're more of a band than we've ever been, I must grudgingly admit and our shows actually feel like rock shows for the most part and not the shambolic exercises in noise and velocity. Not always, though—like any and every band, we've occasionally found ourselves in places we really don't belong, the most recent being a rent paying gig at the palace of nouveau riche Boston Jewry, Sidney Hill Country Club.

If you've never heard of the place, I'm not surprised. Only a suburban Jew or a neighbor to the joint would know of its existence. It's gaudy and gauche and probably to any person of taste and refinement or piety, somewhat obnoxious in its New World pretension. Swaths of cheap, purple almost watery velvet fabric are draped at the entryways like those of a movie set to "The Sheik" or any comical take of some house of pasha. Muy uglito. As are the surly valet parker's. The best way to describe it is that it encapsulates everything Phillip Roth said about such people and places in "Goodbye Columbus" or "Portnoy's Complaint" and I guarantee you I am the only member of Thrills (as the band's only non-gentile) to have perused those hoary tomes.

We owed rent on our rehearsal space and didn't have it and the kindly if eccentric and hyper-manic owner of same suggested we pay it off by playing a party at this chateau. That we didn't fit the bill of anything the place had ever seen being a punk band mattered nothing, I suspect his true aim was to freak out his peers the same way someone with a pet Komodo Dragon in his pool might freak out theirs.

OK, you want us to be the freely sprung asylum denizens off their Thorazine and out of their confines, you got it, pal. Oh, did we ever ham it up to the extreme and no one danced a single beat, they just stood and stared at us, as if that giant inflatable phallus Jagger used on the Stones tours had casually sauntered onto the makeshift stage and was gyrating away with the band. For the coup de grace, El Senor Angel rammed the neck of his Strat through the ceiling while doing a deranged tango atop a dining table as the band simmered through "Kicking Cripples" behind him, a song we generally no longer performed as we're "serious", but we're also in on this gag, too.

I can't believe the place's management didn't have us lined up against the wall and shot like South American renegades. They were enraged. I reckon Jeffrey, the rehearsal space owner greased their palms to cover the actual damages we did to the venue and with the assurances that he had no idea we'd do what we did, that he too was completely floored and would sternly deal with us in his own way.

He said nothing and winked at me on the way out the door. It was a great prank pulled on these stuffed shirt, spoiled brat sons and daughters of Israel, the ultimate fuck you and made him even more punk rock than we were!

However, by this point in the band's life, if there was one female possibility in the room for Johnny's amusement and pleasure, I would zero in on her like a laser and at this total washout of a farce, I miraculously succeeded. One of the music students at the school Jeffrey ran was this beautiful, almond eyed exotica from the distant land of Marblehead. Sort of like a non-shiksa Dee. She spoke in this tiny, incredibly shy but deep voice and introduced herself as Audrey — just like Hepburn, am I lucky or what?

Audrey had this attic place in Brookline not too far from the country club and boldly (for an 18 year old suburbanite) asked me if I'd like to spend the night with her there. Why not ask if I'd like the sky to rain hundred dollar bills, my dear? Of course.

Her little bed was right under the slant of the roof, shoved in the corner of the place and I kept smacking my ass against the thing on the upstroke as we kanoodled away. She was slender and soft and dark haired and just plain heavenly, one of the really marvelous things about the nascent punk scene was that there wasn't a type of person or a stereotype of a person drawn to it and its freedoms, it included anyone, even this fresh out of high school doll.

Me being me, I am never that content offstage, even when plunging myself into paradise, penis first. So, when Audrey and I took a pause between the lapping and pounding, I decided to do a little kooky kabuki for her benefit.

Climbing out of her bed (carefully as not to dent my cranium), I sauntered over to the middle of her room and proceeded to do cartwheels across the raggedly floor. Her big eyes widened and she was desperately trying not to giggle at the sight of the mop-topped punk playing cheerleader, only nude and erect.

She smiled widely and made the universal gesture of tongue in cheek bobbing in and out with accompanying fist (as in "get over here, I feel a blow job coming on") and the floor show was over.

. . . .
.

And as absurd as that one night was, there were so many of them that only the sheer level of absurdity makes it stand out. We were becoming this peculiar underground-headed-to-the-surface phenomenon and what can happen next, we don't know.

So the pressure is on at this point, with a genuine fan base and radio hit and our first trip to NYC deemed a success (if not a suck-cess, I am awful, I admit it) and we're going back. Barb's boss at the radio station, WBCN, has hooked us up with a pair of serious biz pro heavyweights, one of whom produced the Dead Boys and the other one of my absolute avatars and gurus, the former lead guitar player from the Spiders From Mars. Allegedly, they're gonna have some imprint label distributed by CBS and they're impressed by our single, or more accurately, Barb's mellifluous singing, a rarity for the kind of music that backs her. Cool. I have no jealousy issues with Barb at all--to paraphrase the great poet, she's my ticket to ride and I don't care. (And I think the rhythm section agrees). Good thing she sings so well, because she is such a ball busting little pain in the ass, turning up later and later for practices and becoming less Patti and more Liza Minelli in her hauteur.

So, we're back on the 95 to Manhattan and not quite as out of it the second time around and much better prepared to boot. I'll be cribbing with Donna for real, with that walrus chopped old hippie ex of hers now out the door, consummation is indeed in the cards. The others have also staked out crash pads up and down the island and this time, it's not a rock disco we're at, but the sacred shrine itself, CBGB.

As tourist and out of town wide eyed gawker as we still are, we're cognizant of the fact that 315 Bowery has already seen better days. When I'd haul ass down to the city in '77 as a goggle-eyed fan-boy, I felt immersed in my people like this was the Ellis Island of punk rock itself. Now, it seemed like a little of the air had been sucked out of the place. The NYC hangout vibe seems like it had made like a garden snake and was probably under a new rock that we didn't know about.

But it's still CB's and we've decided to play every one of our songs over the four sets for this showcase to give the producer pair a fair shot. Finally meeting the female half of the crew at the club, she informs us that she's going to tape the sets. This sets alarm bells off in Barb's defensive and tipped-to-paranoia head about rip-offs and she slams her tiny little feet into the floor of the club in refusal. Why she did this is a mystery to me, I am the author of the material and someone with no objections, but Barb holds her ground and refuses to go onstage until Genya the Producer promises not to tape. What Barb in her tunnel-vision insanity doesn't get is that we hold no aces and it isn't gonna make Genya want to work with us, let alone Mick Ronson. We are losing already.

And we board that stage and the sound is ripping and we tear it up, even running through tunes Barb hates like "Queen of Cool" and there are a handful of expats from New England upfront and it's like being back in mama's arms a bit. Except the one I have been craving for a month is nowhere to be seen, Ms Dee. I have this unshakable faith that things always proceed to their logical end and that includes the prospect of both Donna and Dee at CB's at the same time and what will I do, cue that old Lovin' Spoonful tune, "Did You Ever Have To Make Up Your Mind", right? I ain't worried, whatever happens happens (OK, DON'T cue Doris Day and "Que Sera Sera", I have limits). Besides, who knows-- the possibility of a menage might even loom and it's a good thing I don't ruminate on that one too much of I'd forget all the chords to all my songs!

Donna there, Dee, no. We're playing here tomorrow anyway, maybe Dee will be here, she does scan the Village Voice like a trained falcon over a valley filled with mice, she's gotta know I'm here. Two sets and a hang with Charlie and Donna and a few others and Genya is nowhere to be seen. As I have been pounding Buds since a little past Hartford for the last 7 hours, I'm a little anxiety immune but I'm thinking we fucked up big time here with Barb's little snit having shut the door on that deal now looking like a sure thing. Oh well, collect our twenty bucks a piece and off to uptown and Donna's.

Whatever miseries one endures or whatever feelings of existential terror drift through a mind, they sure evaporate like a desert mist in the morning does when the matter of pussy rears its pink and perfect head. And Donna's is welcoming and ready the way hot cocoa is in a January blizzard, when you get out of that snow and sopped winter gear and mama's love is served up in a steaming mug. Except better, like a velvet glove wrapped around you, and as Donna is a bit of a love n kisses type as opposed to a pound the crap out of me, daddy type, I have forgotten all about the disaster downtown. At least for now. She is cooing to me, sweetly asking me to call her "darling" and sweetheart", which, being all the way inside her, isn't the most unreasonable request as I'm feeling that too.

She seems a little curt and cold and cut short the next day, though. Maybe because she's working or more likely because in her mind, her better judgment took a vacation and as a result, she is an out of town fling for a cocky and irresponsible fellow, namely me. Which, with the glow of alcohol, rock and horniness literally belonging to yesterday, means vamoose fast if you're me and I am and scram I do.

You know, screw protocol and waiting and chance, I'm going to Dee's. She has a pad in Chelsea on West 20th and I got the addy off her last time (no phone though, I am not known as the "Prince of Doing Things Half Assed" for nothing). I reckon by two, she's gotta be up, even after Max's closed and after hours places open, two hours past noon is a good bet, true?

I was right, as it turns out. She buzzes me in but doesn't answer her door until I identify (intercom failure in these cruddy flats is as common as break-ins), undoes the chain and police lock and stands before me in a hole-riddled Sex Pistols tee shirt and grubby if still skin tight black Levi's.

"It's so good to see you, baby", I say as I lean forward and get cheek and no lips and a mouthful of last night's slept in powder. She sort of turns and quarter smiles me back.

"It's good to see you too, Johnny, what's up?"

She isn't even surprised I'm there. Not in New York not in Chelsea and not in her foyer. And even if it was only four weeks since I last saw her, she's different, something is off here. Maybe it's because I only saw her in the muted lighting of

Broadway and 64th and now it's the harsh half sunlight of a West Side afternoon, but she isn't Dee as I know her. The sass and spark is tamped down like when coals go grey to ash, which fits her to a tee as she too is ashen. And frail. And unwound, like I'm seeing an abstract rendering of her as opposed to the woman herself. She just doesn't seem here.

"I played CB's last night, where were you?" I still can't get over the blase lack of register here.

"Oh, I never go there anymore, that place is done and besides, they're a little weird with me there", she says and that familiar half smile finally reappears, albeit on badly cracked lips whose stick smear is also still there from the night before.

"Yeah?"

"Yeah", she says and shrugs a "well, what can you do" semi-pirouette. "I ODed at the front door there a few weeks ago and sorta went out on the street, some really good shit had come into town that week and I didn't know it".

I nodded sagely as if to say 'well shit like that happens" in a semi-sympathetic understanding mode, but really in a horrified and saddened mode. There was now no way to get that train back on its track, the idea that she and I should be together because this development was not the Dee I saw in my mind and the one standing in front of me was the actual one, the battered butterfly out of the cocoon, the one-time admirer of street toughs now a dues paying member in good standing. And I didn't want that, in my mind, she was Dee, my prospective baby, who I wanted to wake up next to and sing to, because for all of my affected punk personas, I am a believer in true love and up until this minute, I thought she could be it.

"So, she says, after lighting a cigarette, deftly blowing out the match-head with a lung full of bluish smoke, "they put me in an ambulance and I was stuck in Bellevue for three days lockdown. What a bunch of freaks, Johnny". And draws another haul of smoke and eases it out through that pixie-ish snout of hers, with an unmistakable patina of pride.

"So, you wan' some coffee, I gotta make up a pot?"

"Sure", I say and sit down on her couch and no sooner do I take a load off than at least twenty fleet footed cockroaches scurry off the battered boxed springs and threadbare cushions and into the corner. I've lived in cities for the last 3 years and never seen an insect farm quite as revoltingly impressive as Dee's menagerie of vermin, there was even a family of what appeared to be albino roaches, like long strands of running Uncle Ben's making for the darkness.

Dee returns with a pair of cups, ciggy dangling off her lips and giggling a bit. "Don't freak out over them, Johnny, they're bugs, you're a big strong man, they can't hurt you." And on the "you", the coffin nail drops off her lips onto her pocked floor and she quickly stamps it out.

More small talk. I have always kept a little distance from Dee because I have sensed, like I say, she could really hurt me. But now it's different. My armor and guard is up because she is someone else. She may have crossed over into the land of wasted scene-girl and I have been hit and running those women for years and never feeling anything for them other than very temporary lust at best. I'm debating whether or not to get to know and love this new Dee like I did the old one or just write her off as another dippy rock casualty girl whose drug dabbling made them an unappealing, barely walking disaster. It is already tearing me apart, like Ali and Foreman are duking it out just south of my esophagus.

But I ain't letting on. Not now and not ever. I tell her I gotta get to the Bowery for sound-check and she says she'll see me there. No problem.

But this second night of the stand is an abomination. Two bands that were pals with CB's owner Hilly Kristal to get this Saturday gig have crowbarred their way on to the bill and our midnight set is now at 2:30AM. As wired as we are to play, there's no label people that we can see and after the two local acts are done, their regulars slither away to the back of that long railroad flat bar to the front and the street. Our people are long gone, too. And all we see is the slow fade and shuffle of the last few tables towards the door, as we gamely bang out our set.

About 2/3's of the way through, I remember that Dee promised she'd show. And between a few numbers, as Barb takes a pull of her beer and Merle tunes and Mike tightens his snare head, I shade my eyes from the stage lights overhead and peer into the emptying room, vexed and perplexed and now with a tsunami of disappointment crashing down on me.

There's no Dee.

"Hey", I yell into the mic. "There seems to be somebody absent. Someone's supposed to be here and is fucking not. Hello, hello--looking for Dee. Where's Dee, Paging Dee. Looking for Lady Dee".....

Chapter 12/Boston /June/1979.

There's nothing I learned in any school I ever went to, be it elementary schools to junior high to high school to the informal loony bin alternative high school my mom sent me to across the street from the Rat to college that could have prepped me for what happened in the summer and fall. What would the class have been? "Complete Chaos Crash and Burn 101"? "Intro to Mind-fuck"?

If it were someone else's life, I'd be howling with laughter. Because it's mine, it perches me on the precipice of one of my anxiety attacks every time I think on it too much. I better spit it out step by step then.

Shortly after returning from CB's and Dee's too much junkie business, I got to go to my first "press event", for the singer Lene Lovich. She had come to see us at the Rat the night before and was impressed enough to proffer an invite to us to join her at the Hyatt the next night for a CBS Records meet n greet. I'd never been on the invited list for anything before—you might say this aspect of my social life was like being picked last for kickball all over again. Why none of the others went is a mystery but upon discovering the open hotel bar, I couldn't believe my good fortune. Free booze as far as the eye can see and belly up to the bar till I am belly up.

With my schoolmate Lauren as date, we began the ritual brain cell demolition that only an endless river of double Scotches can provide. I have no memory whatsoever of Lene or for that matter anything else save a lengthy argument in the men's room with a local writer for the Boston Globe, a kindly and bemused lad named Jim Sullivan. Having become completely alkie gonzo, it was only Jim that wanted to endure the slippery tongued salvos of the bombed bard. Lauren split utterly furious and in what may have been a millisecond of clarity, I realized she had vanished and implored my new friend to get me over to the Rat in double time, where I assumed she was.

I guessed right. Onstage this Monday night were the Dawgs, four of the greatest, sweetest and absolutely Boston's North Shore towniest boys you'd ever want to know and Lauren was semi-enjoying them as I breezed past her dazed to join them onstage (uninvited) to bellow out "(I Can't Get No) Satisfaction". Badly and horizontal. Why they didn't kick the piss out of me I'll never know (they were that gentle hearted) but I was hauled offstage by Thrills roadie Jimmy who carried me up those slippery metal steps to the back where I proceeded to projectile puke all over a line of automobiles. They're now newly redecorated with Scotch and Johnny bile. Hey no charge!

Carrying me back down the same stairs ten minutes later, I broke Jimmy's foot. I learned this a week after the date.

Lauren was justifiably furious but she was also determined to get something out of this badly aborted get together and literally hauled me four blocks to her place on Beacon Street and lo and behold, my legs didn't work and I couldn't see or speak but praise the fates SOMETHING rose from the depths of my presently distilled spirits. When all else failed, the primal urge conquered my liquor saturated self and amazingly. HE WAS RISEN.

She didn't speak to me the next day. Which would have been an absolute disaster of a hangover day had I not gotten the news that Thrills had landed two nights at the Paradise opening for our saviors, the Ramones.

I was floating above my body. See, I never ever had dreams or plans or wishes, I just wanted a hassle free existence from cradle to grave, just to be able to be in my cloud of self-directed fantasy. I aspired to no higher goal. But with all of these astonishing events coming at me like asteroids in the cosmos, I was just free falling through it or maybe pin-balling, as a pinball careens down a machine? All musicians do that, I've found but the thing is, a pinball has no central nervous system and feels no pain or ecstasy, people do and when those flippers send you up, it's at glorious warp speed but as you the human pinball descend or the machine tilts you, oh you know it hurts in the ignominious landing.

Plus, Thrills were the favorites to win this contest Barb's old station was putting on, a "rock and roll rumble" and our preliminary night was a few days before the first show with the Ramones. That battle of the bands was all anyone could talk about, especially with us landing the Holy Grail of support gigs concurrent with it. The "serious band" thing was in hyper-drive.

We won our night easily and two days later loaded in to the Paradise to share the evening with the gods themselves. Our name proudly beneath theirs on the marquee and if this isn't the big time, what is?

Generally, bands that supported the Ramones had a tough time, but because we were seen as their baby brother band, the audience was all revved up and ready to go from the first notes of the set and hopping by the third song. The fourth tune being our drone fuzz bomb one chord wonder "When Ya Gonna Quit?", I stroked out the intro, reared back to where my amp was and made a spectacular leap to the front of the stage.

Leap was indeed impressive but when the heel of my Cuban-heeled shoe caught the edge of the stage carpeting upon touchdown, my foot stopped cold as the body lurched sideways and my right knee went as if I'd been hit by a 200 lb. free safety. I had no idea what it was. Gamely, I picked myself up and three times I fell and rose as the knee swelled to grapefruit size and couldn't support my weight. I hopped off the stage and pulled myself up the railing to the dressing room.

What a scene. My mom, the retired RN and proud as the proverbial peacock of her semi-notorious son on one side of the damaged limb and Dee Dee Ramone MD on the other, offering their respective advice (Dee Dee had slammed a car door on his a few weeks earlier). It was a scene right out of an acid test and me and my ex Kim, who I was seeing for the first time in three years limped off to Beth Israel for an X-ray. No broken bones. We repaired to the Queensbury Street digs and as was the case with Lauren, everything else was shut down except the libido and its agent. Next night, I played seated on a stool and did so again two days hence at the Rumble's semi-finals. With no bouncing Johnny, Thrills had no onstage energy and lost badly to the sparked up and psyched out Neighborhoods. After the announcement of defeat, the J Geils Band did an impromptu set there but at that point, I could have cared less. This summer was a bummer already.

Not completely. The knee healed enough to walk on. And the deserted city as I spoke of before-- when it gets that eerie vibe about it, the remaining inhabitants get a little loopy, not unlike a tribe of moon besotted werewolves.

Case in point was a little house party I found myself at where the Public Gardens meet the mouth of Commonwealth Ave. Already thirty three sheets to the wind upon arrival, it was a plethora of Emerson College classmates (I was a marginal student there, staying precariously out of my worst nightmare, a day-job) and I was glad to see all of them through my bloodshot eyes, especially an on again off again lady pal, Madelyn. I had met her a year earlier when she was a coat check girl at one of the local hovels we were playing at and we had a glorious after hours tete a tete then and frequently after. Mad mad Madelyn was quite fond of this sort of activity, as I found out later she'd banged more or less all of my friends.

We exchanged pleasantries and she suggested we go out onto the brownstone's stoop facing the avenue. Good idea--despite indulging in every other vice, smoking had always escaped me appeal wise and the haze in the flat was burning pockmarks in my retinas. So, we sat on the top step watching the cars go by perhaps 15 or 20 feet in front of us when she decides she'd like to give me a blow job right then and there. In clear sight of one of Boston's busiest corners, Comm. Ave and Arlington St.

Don't get the wrong idea after all these admissions of emission, public sex is way too tense and loans itself to a level of discomfort I can't take if I'm gonna let all the way go. Even utterly blotto. So, somewhere in the back of my mind, I realized this was not such a great idea after all, pulled her head off my dong and out of my lap and steered us indoors.

But we were pumped and I somehow slid her into the bathroom where we proceeded to fuck full on wild-style on the floor. Aside from her pretty blond head slamming into the toilet every fourth thrust, it was going quite well until Madsy lost her cool and started screaming with joy. Sobering up rapidly, it occurred to me that someone was going to bust down the door suspecting an assault/murder in progress if I didn't quiet her down, but as she was pulling my hips up and down like a laundry bag being shaken into a washer, it wasn't like I could stop. So, sensible man that I am under pressure, I reached over and turned the shower on, full blast. Problem solved. Madelyn now inaudible.

I forgot to turn it off when we zipped up and left, though. What an ungodly mess. The resulting flood was local legendary.

Never got asked back there again.

Some high point. But in the fall, we rose. Not quite all the way back to "local darlings hood"-- that belonged to the Neighborhoods now--but we landed two incredible shows within a few days of each other. The first was supporting hero #2 Mr. Johnny Thunders at a small club in Cambridge. The second was in support of the now massive Cars at a 4500 seat venue on the day the Pope was to speak on the Commons.

The former gig was a catastrophe. Thunders had brought no amp to the show, nor had his band-mate on lead guitar, Wayne Kramer, formerly of the MC5. I got a call from my horrid ex at home after sound-check, she took it upon herself as Thunders' new aide de camp to find the virtuoso some gear. Not mine, honey--he was notorious for blowing shit up at Max's and I was four days from the biggest gig of my life. So, it was pins and needles tense back at the venue.

Which escalated when I saw a woman that I had invited to the gig, Elissa, carrying a tray of drinks into their dressing room. When I asked her who they were for, she told me. So, I asked if she was a waitress there now, she said no, and I sent the tray flying, booze and ice filling the air like shrapnel. No one chumps my friends by playing the star card, I told her and this rare display of misplaced chivalry impressed her enough so that during Thunders/Kramer's set, we spent most of it lip locking on the grimy dance floor.

Which continued all the way back to the 700 Tower, Boston University's main dorm. I was much smitten by this kitten (she had the most beautiful green eyes I'd ever seen) and because I could be the greatest salesman ever when the issue of impending intercourse was on the table, she was conned into breaking rules and having me up to her room. About 4 AM or so, I really had to relieve myself and damn it this is an all-girls floor. Being somewhat still potted, I simply rolled out of her bed and sauntered casually down the hall to the can, schlong swinging in rhythm with my steps and unencumbered by jeans. This caused the two women that also needed to use the facilities to jaw drop but I made polite chatter, washed my hands and scooted out of the bathroom and to her little room before they could call the guards.

Four days later, Thrills are nervously waiting backstage at the Boston Music Hall. Well, me less than them because in my twisted thinking, the Cars had been one of the most tepid, lifeless live bands I'd ever witnessed at the Rat and we, why, we were Thrills, baby! We were gonna send them home a whimpering! That they had a half dozen radio hits and had sold all the tickets at that point was meaningless, we were fun! Plus, the whole place was ready to explode--getting into the city had been rendered nearly impossible with public transportation shut down for the Pontiff's visit. We'd had to haul our gear the day before by taxi, as that part of town was closed to all vehicles.

Of the 4500 or so people there, maybe a hundred of them had ever seen a punk band. And there was nothing during what few pauses we took--not a sound. Barb and Merle panicked a little by the huge pillow of darkness in front of us, a room that size means you can't see anyone's face, but I figured, I'll make them remember--Pete Townshend windmills, flying kicks, somersaults, climbing the PA. Watch ME work, suckers.

Nothing. At the end of the set, it sounded like a wall of mooing bovines. "MOOOOO". I asked Ben

Orr, the Cars leering and grinning bass player why they were doing that, because maybe "cars" sounds like "cows"?

"Oh no, they're not mooing, Johnny", he replied, beaming across that big wide face of his. "They're booing--they hated you". And then handed me a towel. Good man.

"But we were good, man".

"I thought so", he said. "But don't take it personally--when Suicide opened for us, the audience tried to kill them!"

Small consolation.

A week later, we gigged with the Ramones again at their local premiere of "Rock and Roll High School". No injury this time. Great show. And headed out for a week of gigs in Michigan.

Booked by a few friends of ours back there, we did five shows in six days to maybe a hundred people total in the Motor City. It was a costly waste of time atop a sixteen hour drive. Other than seeing Sonic's Rendezvous Band, paying for shit through bulletproof plexiglass, sipping Vernor's for the first time and meeting the vivacious "queen of Detroit", Ms. Becky Sharp, it wasn't too great and nearly fatal. We got lost coming back from a gig one night, me and our roadie Gameshow (his real name is Tom Kennedy, same name as the game show host, hence, Merle's nickname for him) and might have been badly hurt in that city were I not so out of it inebriated. We stopped at a diner in this neighborhood called Cass Corridor at about three AM to get directions back to Eight Mile Road and after I ambled into the joint, the sheer bewilderment that this white skinned dummy was adrift in the ghetto just paralyzed the locals with laughter. I laughed too. They laugh, I laugh. We all laugh together. Never crossed my sizzled brain pan that the reason for their jocularity was that no white folks—and certainly no punk rocker white folks—were ever there after sunset. Gameshow, not laughing, was crying, his face in his hands in the car, praying that the brothers didn't just decide to off us right there for shits and giggles. I didn't even know what had really happened till the next day at breakfast. Yikes!

This idea that life on the road is romantic and you pay your dues and it is all good, brothers and sisters? That's shit. Four people to see you 700 hundred miles from home is the most painful reminder in the world that outside the goldfish bowl you are very much "another face in the crowd".

Except there's no crowd.

When I got home after driving all night and day with Merle through Canada and upstate New York, I staggered into Elissa's arms and found she and I had enough change to buy a pizza that had to last three days. This was the first time it had ever hit me--maybe just maybe this isn't going to happen and for Thrills, maybe the thrill was gone. I'd never felt that way before about the band. And I got the sense that I might not be shaking it off so easily in the future, either.

Chapter 13/Facebook/Cyberspace/September 2013.

VIVDeMILO: Hey you!

JOHNNYANGELWENDELL: Get off of my cloud?

VIVDeMILO: LOL...everything is a song to you, isn't it?

JOHNNYANGELWENDELL: Indeed it is, oh lovely one. News updates on the Dee battlefront?

VIVDeMILO: Nothing. Lexis turns up nothing on Dee McClain, anywhere in upstate New York. I have the right birthday but the parents don't have a daughter named Dee, the ones I think they were.

JOHNNYANGELWENDELL: Hmmm....what about the presumed brothers?

VIVDeMILO: One is out west and one is in Maryland.

JOHNNYANGELWENDELL: What does the one in Maryland do?
VIVDeMILO: Lawyer.
JOHNNYANGELWENDELL: Is that the one that won't answer you on FB?
JOHNNYANGELWENDELL: Stonewall McClain?
VIVDeMILO: Yes.
JOHNNYANGELWENDELL: Well, you won't like this, but this may be what you gotta do, Viv: Get on up there, make an appointment with him on some pretext, like a family member has an estate there. Then, ask the fucker point blank about Dee.
JOHNNYANGELWENDELL: And that new profile photo of you...whew. How come you don't post more pics of yourself?
VIVDeMILO: I take other people's photos. Mine, no.
JOHNNYANGELWENDELL: Jobs lately?
VIVDeMILO: Yes, a rally, "Florida Mothers Against Gun Violence" in J-Ville.
JOHNNYANGELWENDELL: An anti-gun rally in Florida? What was that, like eight housewives protesting and 400 fat, bald, open carry thimble dicked white men yelling at them?
VIVDeMILO: LMFAO!!!! Oh no, nothing like that-- just a few moms waving plastic pistols about in the air, I'll send you the proofs when they're done.
JOHNNYANGELWENDELL: Cool thing.
JOHNNYANGELWENDELL: So, once again. Why didn't you ever introduce yourself back then when

you were Dee clubbing? What did you think I was gonna do, bite your face off?

VIVDeMILO: That seemed like a distinct possibility.

JOHNNYANGELWENDELL: Oh of course not. We all fronted back then. I was so transparently a lightweight, though. Amazed I fooled anyone.

VIVDeMILO: You were a terrifying sight, all angry and scowling and pouting. Very cute though.

JOHNNYANGELWENDELL: Oh? Do tell?

VIVDeMILO: Oh come on now. You and the other boys Dee liked always had girls surrounding you in packs.

JOHNNYANGELWENDELL: But she always got us. And it wasn't like she was persistent. She just had that thing, that "it". You probably did too.

VIVDeMILO: Now I AM blushing, Mr. Wendell.

JOHNNYANGELWENDELL: OFFS, ViV. No way.

VIVDeMILO: OFFS?

JOHNNYANGELWENDELL: oh for fucks sake.

VIVDeMILO: LOL.

VIVDeMILO: I really have to go all the way to Baltimore. Really?

JOHNNYANGELWENDELL: Mos def---he isn't gonna talk to you online, but if he's a typical attorney, just squeezing a billable hour from you will make him soil his boxers in ecstasy.

VIVDeMILO: LOL again. You are killing me, Johnny.

JOHNNYANGELWENDELL: Then I'll need McClain to defend me in court, right?

VIVDeMILO: I give up. That brain of yours. Goodness!

JOHNNYANGELWENDELL. Badness. OK--go make an appointment with the ambulance chaser and corner the fuck and tell me what he says, k?

VIVDeMILO: k.

VIVDeMILO: Oh yeah—guess who sent me a friend's request here?

JOHNNYANGELWENDELL: The cast of "Friends"?

VIVDeMILO: LOL, no. Creepy old Nick Rowland.

JOHNNYANGELWENDELL: You have to be joking.

VIVDeMILO: No, sad to say. Should I?

JOHNNYANGELWENDELL: I suppose—keep your friends close and keep your enemies closer although not so close that they give you crabs and you need A-200. I can't believe that ancient, slobbering wretch of a baby rapist isn't dead or in prison.

VIVDeMILO: Point taken and colorfully so.

JOHNNYANGELWENDELL: Speaking of which, I got a friend's request yesterday from this really strange chick back in the day, Sally. Really a trip, a hardcore punker chick from the first wave, like when you and Dee were coming around—I took her back to my place once and while I was sleeping, she gave me head and when I was "up" snapped a polaroid of it!

VIVDeMILO: Are you kidding me, that's awful, what a violation of privacy.

JOHNNYANGELWENDELL: That wasn't the worst of it. She shared the thing with everyone she knew, they passed it around like it was a photo of a rare Egyptian hieroglyphic or the Shroud of Turin or something. I would never have known about it if that DJ guy, the gay one in the afternoon's hadn't told me about it—that fuck actually told me that he'd never played us on his show but now we could be featured if I just let him have a peep in person.

VIVDeMILO: And did you?

JOHNNYANGELWENDELL: Hey, I was cheap but not easy. OK, I was cheap and easy. But I had my standards. OK, I had no standards. But no, I never did. Years later, walking down Park Drive, early evening, I did moon him—he was leaning out his window and gave me this "hey, Johnny" greeting and I yelled back "happy birthday, motherfucker" and dropped these denim shorts I had on. I was so shitfaced. And yeah, he played the Blackjacks, ya know, the band after Thrills after that ass dance every fucking afternoon!

VIVDeMILO: If you could see me, you'd see I am nearly doubled over. Did you bring that up with her? The photo I mean, not the inebriated strip tease for the gay-boy.

JOHNNYANGELWENDELL: Yeah, why not? Me and Sally laughed it off. She's been a clean single mom for over fifteen years now, she says. I can't be mad at her and besides, she invented the selfie!!!!!

VIVDeMILO: LOL. Oh my, my head hurts, you're killing me.

JOHNNYANGELWENDELL: I do my best.

VIVDeMILO: And on that humble note, I must go.

JOHNNYANGELWENDELL: Me too.

JOHNNYANGELWENDELL: xxxooo. bye.

VIVDeMILO: bye.

Chapter 14/Havre De Grace, Maryland/October 2013.

The rolling hills of northern Maryland between the Baltimore suburbs and the Delaware border may be the most beautiful terrain in the US. Gentle slopes of varied grassiness, this is horse country with many stables turning out champion thoroughbreds dotting the landscape, the genteel, bucolic anesthetic of old money is draped over the countryside like a narcotic miasma. No matter how many times anyone travels the I-95 in either direction, it's a blessed relief after the industrial ugliness of downtown Baltimore in one direction and the carbuncle that DuPont built, Delaware, in the other.

Which makes it the perfect address for Robert C. McClain, attorney at law, estates a specialty, probate. A tubby, red-faced country lawyer with a large shock of blond comb-over and crimson proboscis, he bears an uncanny resemblance to William Weld, Massachusetts' former governor and also the uber-WASP prototype to which McClain aspires. That reserved, studied immovable wall of emotionless stone-facedness with more than a little learned semi-southern good old boyism to fit in with the locals here slightly north of the Mason Dixon line, he's done quite well for himself. Especially after his conversion to Baptism and the "born again" eureka experience which pulled him from the bottom of the Jack Daniels bottle some 14 years earlier.

Sitting in the lobby of his Havre De Grace red-bricked office is Viv DeMilo, who, on the recommendation of J. A. Wendell, has toned down her artist in exile appearance. Her blond mane tied neatly behind her ears and the only business suit she owns, a serge blue number that made her itch draped over her bones. Flat, bland slip-over shoes too, no heels or Docs or Chucks today. The things we do to get a straight answer out of people, she ponders, I'm paying two hundred dollars for an hour of his time and I have to impress him? Seems nonsensical.

But as someone whose livelihood is the portrait of the oddball and the even keeled, she is a people watcher with a keen sense of intuition. The harried, texting, agitated fellow that has proceeded her at the office, she has sussed out that he is getting a serious ass-raping from his ex as per child support or alimony, years of work have given her the most important insight of her life--what you see in front of you rarely lies, it's the words that do. The way someone looks at you, the reserve of their smile, how the shoulders sit-- her camera catches all of it and she is rarely wrong even when not on the other side of the lens.

A couple of minutes after this poor wretch races out of the attorney's office, McClain's door opens and McClain walks over to where Viv is seated, lips stretched across his teeth in what might charitably be called a smile, a business-like one, anyway. Viv stands to shake his hand and thinks to herself, this guy is barely above room temperature. Could he really be Dee's brother?

"Bob McClain--you are Miss DeMilo? Or is it Mrs. DeMilo?"

It's "Ms" thinks Viv, but that kind of correction won't help the cause at all and she can hear Johnny's voice in the back of her head repeating "eyes on the prize" like an invocation.

"It's "miss", thanks, good to meet you too, Mr. McClain". And he steers her into his inner sanctum and into the comfort of a deep black leather seat facing his desk. Great--now Johnny's voice is gone and all I can hear is "rich Corinthian leather" from Ricardo Montalban, she thinks. The thought of that forces her to bite her lips and she can feel a major smirk coming on--not now, Viv. Tell your punk rock side to take a brief hike.

"So, what can I do for you today", he asks. What he really means is "how much legal foolishness has your family incurred that I can insert myself into the middle of", but that goes without saying.

"You told me that your family left you an estate outside of town and that there may be some lien issues that need to be addressed?"

Johnny's younger brother is an attorney and has suggested that one to reel the marlin McClain in.

"Well, yes, Mr. McClain", she responds. "But I am most interested in your family first, I feel that to do business with anyone, one must know their background". Touche. Having done her homework (or more accurately, Johnny had), she knows that the route to this particular truth has to be negotiated through the lingua franca of the born again Christian and family is her best bet, not to mention the quickest. Gumming with him about Jesus could last all day and bankrupt her.
"Well, I am an open book, I suppose", says the mouthpiece, leaning back into his chair, hands folded behind his balding head. "I am a happily married man with two lovely daughters and a grandson, we live about a mile outside downtown Havre. Does that sufficiently answer you, ma'am?"

"What about your upbringing, brothers, sisters, parents?"

Were McClain not too laser-beam focused on making this pretty little thing a temporary goldmine he could drain of money he might have been justifiably weirded out by this query, but gamely, he answered. "My father is no longer with us, mother is in upstate New York and I have two brothers".

Shit.

"No sisters?"

"No. Why are you asking me that?" There's a bit of agitation in his voice. He's never answered this sort of line of questioning and he's dealt with millionaire attorneys in court from DC all the way to San Fran.

"Well", says Viv, thinking quickly. "I always prefer to deal with men with sisters, they do seem to understand women a little better, that's just what I have observed, nothing all that important, really." Oh, if she could pat herself on the back for that quick save she would. Right there.

"No, I have no sisters. I had one, a younger sister, Evelyn, but she passed away young".

Evelyn?

"I'm so sorry," Viv intones somberly. "Losing a sibling in childhood is traumatizing, I am so very, very sorry".

"Well", McClain says, sighing audibly through both nose and kisser, "my sister was 27 and had a very rough time in her life. I prefer not to speak of her, she hurt my mother badly and broke my father's heart with the life she chose to live".

"I don't mean to pry, but what did she do that was so awful?"

McClain looked down at the burgundy carpet under his desk, collected himself and looked directly at Viv.

"She turned her back on the lord, Miss DeMilo. She consorted with a crowd of wicked people. I cannot speak more of this, can we discuss the lien's on your late father's estate, please?"

Now or never time, put up or shut up, Viv thought. He's never going to tell me anything, this I'll have to find out on my own and I have to confirm this.

"Did Evelyn call herself another name, Mr. McClain? Like, say "Dee", perhaps?"

At this moment, McClain's face fell. His normally hale rouge-like glow had gone stone granite, as if the patina had been erased.

"Who are you and what do you really want?" He asked.

Viv stood up, coolly and calmly.

"Dee was my friend. Where is she?"

"I do not ever discuss my sister with anyone, especially her cohorts from those awful years. Our meeting is over," he replied curtly. "I don't know or care who you are but I assure you I will speak no more of this and if you do not leave immediately, I'll call the police. Good day and goodbye" And as if he were Jehovah himself, he straightened his arm all the way out, with index finger aimed at the street.

"Why can't you tell me what happened to her", Viv implored, rising to leave. "I'll go, but I have to know what happened?"

"GET OUT", he yelled, loud enough so that his clientele in the lobby were startled and even more so when Viv, coat over shoulder, exited suddenly. She bolted through his glass doors and out to her rental, quickly to the highway and south to Baltimore. She had what she needed now. And in the adrenaline rush that sustained her all the way to the airport, she didn't even stop to grieve the news--Dee was dead.

Chapter 15/Boston/November 1979.

Ms. Pinky Leather never saw herself as a philosopher queen but it didn't stop her from weighing in on the dead end street that our little scene was becoming. Sitting upstairs at the Rat over Long Island Iced Teas, the perpetually eupeptic suburbanite waxed eloquent upon what I've been wishing for myself.

"Wouldn't it be great if everyone got into what we're into," she mused. "Like, it wouldn't just be the same people at every show but if our thing became everybody's thing, it would be like we took over the world". I nod in agreement. That's been my bone to pick for the last five months since I totaled the cartilage in my right knee. I don't want to have to sound like Foreigner or 38 Special to be as big as them, I want to be as big as them sounding like me!

Winter doldrums, which meant the exit of students coupled with brackish, black soot toned slush, were starting to set in. Plus poverty--if Elissa hadn't been lifting a dozen ham and cheese on white bread every few days from BU, I'd have been down to 120 pounds and donating blood. And we of Thrills have made a major decision, my idea, which also is my demotion. I have suggested and then found a genuine lead guitar player among our circle who is more than happy to rave with us.

He's Sean from Connecticut. On Thrills' first road trip, to the exotic wilds of Milford (outside Stamford), we shared a bill with his band and he and I jammed for an hour an sound-check on nothing but Dictators, Ramones, Heartbreakers and Dolls tunes. We brought them (The Survivors) north for a few shows and kept in touch and after the Michigan mishegoss, I realized a change had to be made and stepping down to rhythm guitar in favor of a real soloist would be a fresh injection of fierce new energy.

My guitar playing sucks. There, I said it. I failed every audition I ever had until I started auditioning people for MY band. When punk rock elbowed virtuosity out the door in favor of inspired insanity, I was suddenly chic and got asked to join all kinds of bands, from DMZ to LaPeste. Stung from rejection and stubbornly loyal to Barb, I always declined, but when I masquerade as/imitate a Jimmy Page type noodler, I was and am hopeless and hapless.

Sean was good, a Ross the Boss (of the Dictators) type lead player that adored velocity and distortion and agreed to join us in January 1980. I can't wait to spring him on the world. Plus, he's a ferocious snarling little dude and not a self-involved hippie twiddler. Look out, I think this is gonna be good.

FEBRUARY 1980.

Mixed notices on the new lead guitar. The band is ecstatic to sport all this new raw power but our fans are crinkling up their nostrils at the faint scent of arena rock Sean brings. Unfortunately a new sheriff is in town and this one does not require six-string proficiency.

Since the B-52's became the absolute ultra-mega with the collegiate crowd, Pinky Leather's dictum of wide acceptance for our thing is gaining momentum. But it's a variation on it, with skittering beats and hiccup singing and this odd satori of skinny ties and pastels replacing leathers and black. What sort of began with the commercially tolerable Police or Cars or the god-awful Knack has moved slightly leftward to collide with our mayhem to create this brand new middle with a spiffy new spangled and safe title: New Wave.

To me, that meant a type of offbeat French cinema, but in the lingo of the new breed, it's a kind of acceptable soundtrack to bridge and tunnel dance types now allergic to the dreaded disco which they correctly view as passe. Plus, the last few years or so, disco has returned to its roots as being primarily in the gay clubs as dance music and suburbanites in this neck of the woods wig out over being tarred with the queer brush. They're absolutely flocking to a new club on Landsdowne Street called "Spit". Wicked edgy, huh? In the newest expensive togs off Newbury Street, the former Biff's and Muffy's are now shimmying and writhing to "Dance This Mess Around", this is what appears to be bulldozing us out of the basement bands into extinction. Spit's staff was sort of like a whole crew of aggressive Nick Rowland types, but not as nelly--lots of older fellows that were very look the other way on the matter of younger fellows that wanted to get in the door. That didn't sit too well with me but it really wasn't my affair. Plus, as a local oddball that looked the part, I got in free and drank free there as well, rating what was called a "Spit Power Card", a credit card looking thing that was equally effective to get in their door free and then to chop up lines of yay-yo once inside. The Bolivian Marching Powder was as much a part of that scene as ugly wraparound shades. Grind your teeth to the BEAT!

I should have seen this coming from our gigs last year at Hurrah. Let's face it, when anything "hip" becomes watered down enough for the masses it is already history. Unfortunately, in the eyes of fandom, we garage punks are history simply because we existed before this New Wave eighth note boopity-boo did.

Like all trends, it isn't all of one taste. There are jangling pop bands like Split Enz and synthesizer first groups like Gary Numan. And some of the groups are just plain ace with me like XTC or Squeeze or this new girl group from LA that Elissa got turned on to, the Go Go's. But they were all the whisk of the broom that was sweeping us away and did we ever get the heave ho the night we supported one of these, a ska band from England called Madness.

Fasten your seatbelt, because this story will put you through the windshield of "Thrills' clueless clownery".

Barb in her infinite stupidity, nixed a show with the Pretenders because of the comparison to their female lead singer Chrissie Hynde and opted for this other gig at the same venue I'd demolished my hinge at, the Paradise. I knew nothing of Madness besides their one small radio hit "One Step Beyond" and that they were part of a new thing called "Two Tone" with another one of my chick's favorites, the Specials. They seemed like nice enough blokes at sound-check, but as soon as they heard our wall of guitar rama-lama, they too spun on their shiny heels in disgust. We were not surfing their wave.

To say the gig was a disaster is like saying Hiroshima was too fucking loud and hot in the fall of 1945. For one thing, a few hours before downbeat, Sean and I indulged in a local Mexican eatery's finest and after we sent our plates back to the kitchen for lack of mouth searing peppers, the chef obliged by burying our enchiladas in chili flakes, which the two macho dickheads chowed down in competition with each other.

Unfortunately, the meal's intensity meant a punch in the gut level of cramping and blazing anus for me right before we went on, I barricaded myself in the restroom until I was barely vertical and Sean grimaced and squinched his own rectum shut while onstage. But that was nothing compared to the pointy toe in the scrotum the whole band got from a crowd that six months earlier was pogoing away to us--all of those fuckers were now decked out in pork pie hats and Ivy League suits and standing in front of us cross armed like a let-down schoolmarm, 550 of them. Ready to "skank" to these stern faced Limeys playing "reggae" on after us.

That wasn't a wake-up call. That was a bucket of ice water shot through a cannon into your eyeballs.

JUNE 1980

The first half of this year has not been too kind to us. Our old fans have abandoned us and the new ones, which are all turned on to us from the radio play we get, aren't as fired up hyper-manic. And as the New Wave thing sort of includes us in places where people aren't tired of our act (namely Boston), we've begun to travel a lot through New England and are getting decent if not amazing gigs.

Two stand out amid the dreck. One was in Providence at a small place called the Living Room. Just a wonderful little place that did very much appear to be a living room it probably once was, me and Elissa and the crew arrive and then crank out a decent first set after a local opener, but all is not well in the palace of Thrills. Barb's generally powerful and robust singing voice is shot. She is neither feverish nor fatigued. What she is (and what I'm beginning to realize is an escalating issue) is a ''chipper'', a part time enthusiast of king heroin. The missing of practices, the short temper and the total inability to work except as an occasional club booker virtually scream "dope-fiend", but I am a myopic ostrich at heart and if I don't want to see something, I don't. But now she says there's no second set, the horse has made her hoarse. Well, no second set means maybe no pay and even at a hundred a month rent and a stipend from the grandparents as long as I stay in school at Emerson, I need that lucre.

So, I huddle the boys and we figure to soldier through this doing all the dumb tunes we jam on at the space, when our friends come over and we play, like the folkies probably did in Washington Square, only instead of Odetta or Leadbelly, it's "Chinese Rocks" and "Born Too Loose" and "Anarchy In The UK". Plus the two I sing and maybe whatever comes to me--that makes me the singer and front-man and up the stairs we go, sans real singer.

Gingerly, I kick it in with "Personality Crisis" and then "I Wanna Be Sedated" and this bizarre swirl of whackiness surges through the room. The somewhat enthused New Wave/punky Rhode Islanders are no different than Eagles fans that hear "Hotel California" in a bar; when you're drunk and free from the day job on a Friday night, you hear something you know and love and you explode and man, did they ever--They start smashing into each other, fists in the air and a bunch of them get so carried away, they literally rip the heating vent off the side of the wall and start stomping it to scrap.

Barb hears the commotion from the basement and vaults up the stairs to see total delirium in full effect and her not at the helm of it. Survival instinct kicks in like a pro punter and she leaps on to the stage, seizes the mic and announces that she's back! We return to the planned program of speedy and well-rehearsed originals and the maelstrom calms accordingly.

All the way back to Boston, Elissa and I are looking at each other like "wow, what was that, maybe we don't need Barb as much as I thought".

Fissures and cracks like that add a few more pounds to the anvil of doubt. Damn.

. . . .

The second gig of note was at this absolutely abominable place called the Old Downtown Lounge in Portland, Maine. It was a room off the side of a cocktail bar below the diviest, bedbug riddled edifice you ever could imagine, it was so vile, I slept in my clothes even with the heat cranked. The kind of place where delirium tremens was as common as a stubbed toe.

After a Friday show, I left the hotel post our sets with a friend of a friend to a party out in the damned forest primeval and then made whoopie in the back of her wheels because the hotel was too far away with the hormones blazing to wait. She did accompany me to my sour suite and we continued, but the gallons of cheap booze consumed the night before atop zero sleep sent me on my typical morning road jaunt in a semi-fuzzy dream state.

She was still passed out when I began my ritual city walk. Man needs coffee—like an IV or it or a 100% caffeine enema maybe-- and sweets something fierce to battle back the pounding rhythm of skull and cottonmouth and off the main drag a bit, I spy a 7-11 type joint. As I prepare to make a right turn into the place for (non-Southern) comfort I see this mother and child in the front of a station wagon, parked and waiting. And I do the double take of all time--mama was a typical beat-down, sad-eyed exhausted heap looking middle aged woman in an overcoat, but the child--I kid you not and am not lying--was a pinhead, a real one, with the conical skull and Zippy-like bib.

I may have been hallucinating. I don't discount the possibility. But I swear that's what I saw, on a stack of whatever holy tome I lay me palm upon. I turned around and dashed to the hotel, lunged up the stairs and to the floor where the others were. I started pounding on the doors like fucking Paul Revere warning that the British were coming. Barb and Merle and Sean and Mike and their beau's (mine was back in Boston, ergo the bad behavior in the woods) run into the dingy, disgusting hallway and I breathlessly spread the news.

"I saw a pinhead--a fucking pinhead, a real one, no joke, he was real, I saw him--THEY EXIST".

Maybe Sean got his shit on and ambled down the street, the others were irate at this alarming human alarm. They groaned at me and went back to bed. But when we gigged with the Ramones three months later and I laid the same story on them, those front-running fuckers all nodded in ascent (my band, not them). Johnny and Dee Dee were very impressed--validation!

That was the best gig of the year. 2,000 people half wrecked the place during our set and turned every chair in the room to kindling during theirs. A much needed shot in the arm. A week later, I turned 24 and Ms. Pinky Leather handed me a condom by way of birthday gift. To be used immediately. What are friends for?

OCTOBER 1980

I got a new knee, I got it good.

Surgery. Five days in hospital, cartilage all gone. By the Boston Bruins surgeon. His bedside manner was more glacial and brusque than Johnny Rotten's would be. Maybe I should learn limb cutting. The only part of the ordeal worth relating is that for pre-op, they stuck me in a supply closet, IV dripping in arm but not quite medicated enough to not wonder why I was there. If that isn't punk rock, then what is?

Also, when they wheeled me back to my room and I saw Elissa sitting there waiting like the patient partner of the patient, I sat straight up, wrecked on morphine and cried out "HI KITTY", with eyes bulging out of my head like a Big Daddy Roth caricature. She raced down the corridor to heave, she told me later and didn't visit again and when she realized that I expected to nurse me back to vertical by waiting on my every whim, she rebelled. I think her favorite phrase at the time became "get it yourself". I was on crutches and making the Rat/Spit rounds a few days later and even opened a show one-legged for Stiff Little Fingers, a terrific band of first rate bang and smashers.

As I recuperated, we finished a new record in studio and band finally has a manager, too. He's a good guy if just a little too much from a bygone time and his methods of steering us as such are always congruent with my gut sentiments. For example, we have succumbed to the temptations of the times and gone all poppy ourselves. Four songs tracked at the same place Aerosmith made their first record. Finished five minutes before the Cars took ownership of the building. I say this not to name-drop but to admit this is probably as close to stardom as we're getting.

Our new songs, all written cynically, formulaic and knowingly by me have but one aim--mass acceptance. The best of the batch is this sing songy shuffle called "Sorry" which is a hybrid of "Going to the Chapel of Love", "Help Me, Rhonda" and "Waterloo". Barb detests it, it features a C# above high C which she can barely reach. But it becomes, as a demo tape, the biggest tune we ever had on radio. Naturally, included on record, it's already dated and none of the other three songs get played much.

The band's slow fade into a routine, job kind of thing is also reflected in my relationship with Elissa, who has more or less gotten tired of being girlfriend to the most blatantly unfaithful mate in the Northeast. Despite our cohabitation, the moment she jets off to Miami to see her folks, I am off the reservation poon-crazed. With any and all of the local girls that still fancy me a bit.

This is bad enough but my obvious lack of spine when it comes to turning down an eager beaver (pats himself on back and bows) went into the stratosphere while E herself was right next to me one night. We'd played the Rat and all was fine and dandy New Wave/punk pop wise, but right in front of me the whole show was this pretty blond girl I sort of recognized as a fellow Emersonian. We chatted very briefly after the set and with Elissa not 10 feet from me, I scored her phone and address and guaranteed that I would see her later.

Hey, if Babe Ruth can call a shot into the bleachers with absolute confidence, I can too-- right?

Back at the grimy old dump on Queensbury, I waited for sweetie to get sleepy and then announced I had a new tune in mind and had to walk around with it, in the Fens at 3 AM, to feel its proper pulse. She nodded and then nodded out and out the door I went, to the cab stand a few blocks away and wouldn't you know it, the cabbie was an old neighbor of mine from Wellesley that clearly had fallen on hard times. I give him the address and ask him to meet me in front of the pad in the Bay Village one hour after dumping me off.

Up to blond Suzie's flat, a few niceties and then the routine. You'd think I'd tire of the dire predictability of it all or be happy to have a very pretty and gentle souled soul-mate that adored me, but that same feeling that I got at the beginning of the band, the role reversal, the being pursued instead of being the pursuer, it sets a little adding machine off in my brain that clicked up a new conquest like a broker scoring a new account or a crafty used car salesman unloading a lemon on a sucker, it was that cut and dried-- and this is theoretically love-making we're talking here.

Cabbie John got me at 4:15 and I was home by 4:30, Elissa none the wiser and me with no guilt. I'd have to not think I was an asshole to feel bad about it, but as a scorpion stings the frog that carries him across the river because that's what he does, this is what I do when any woman bats an eyelash in seduction mode at me. The grotesque creature of habit. I should get a name tag that says that.

MARCH 1981

Our cute little purple EP had not resuscitated us as we'd hoped. And for the first time in the band's existence. I begin to see we're in the no man's land of total between-ness.

On the one hand, we really wanted to be pop-stars, a situation completely exacerbated by a date Barb had with that newspaper guy, Jim. He escorted her to the Garden to review Pat Benatar and Barb was spellbound--it couldn't have been the music, which was dullsville hard rock or even Pat's pro-vocal chops, it was that PB was playing to 15,000 and B was playing to 150. And because we'd gotten really proficient as musicians, we were not all the way down the competency scale from Pat's band.

But we were and are what we are, which cannot be changed. You can call it integrity if you like, but I prefer "comfort level", I just plain love sloppy, spilling, distorted chords and chaotic jabs at maybe being on the same beat, I love that unpredictable, unstable lurch. To be so disciplined as to be able to play "Hit Me With Your Best Shot" straight faced just isn't in my DNA.

Just as monogamy isn't. Elissa had finally grown exhausted of the philandering which she knew had to be happening from the gossip she was getting back, the topper being a brief fling with a musician in another band who I was crazy for. We agreed to end it and this set off a booze binge that nearly blinded me, I had no idea how much I leaned on her until she was no longer there--one night, my legs literally would not hold me up anymore, I was so broken down. Half drunken bender and half an anxiety attack over abandonment that I couldn't extinguish with booze. Which led to the absolutely unimaginable.

I stopped drinking.

Not as in heard the voice of the Lord and locked myself away in AA or any of that trite twaddle. No, my last bender (at the time) was with a recent ex of the band's bassist. We were both free and not too happy about it and found each other out and about one night at Spit and because I could drink gratis there (they had these adorable black triangular drink tickets), we got pasted wasted.

As we staggered up Landsdowne Street towards the cab stand in Kenmore in front of Pizza Pad, she was babbling about something and as I nodded in ascent, I turned my face away from her and technicolored the sidewalk with a goodly helping of pastel-colored heave. And kept walking. And after we got out to where she lived, went back to another bar and drank some more until closing time and naturally, made it to her digs and dug in to each other.

Next day, the hangover was spectacularly bad, but also the feeling that this time, it may have been excessive. Although she promised to observe silence, this didn't last and she crowed back to her ex about guess who she slept with. The silence I got wasn't her keeping a secret but total non-communication from him--he literally did not speak to me anymore and I didn't know why for another year, that she'd ratted us out (not satisfied enough pissing off her former boyfriend, she also boasted of the tryst to Elissa, it was Elissa that told me this later). I decided on that day that I could no longer keep the alcohol consumption reasonable and so it just plain stopped. Sort of.

I substituted every substance known by man to alter the brain, from 'ludes to marijuana to all stimulants and narcotics, but my drug of choice with demon alcohol no longer feasible, was nitrous. My best pal at the time was a DJ who had a connection that hipped him to this ludicrous pretext and charade, you pretend you're a baker's assistant and you need a canister of the gear and of course they laid it on you for a few hundred. I sucked down enough of that poisonous vapor to knock out the entire city in the world' biggest dentist's chair until one three day run left me with a fever of about 102 or so on Christmas Day (every time you take a belt of that wheezy shit, your immune system gets pole-axed). Like its soul sister the spirits, I did laughing gas to the point of psycho saturation and only then put the tank down.

We were still a band and determined to plow ahead and our manager, who had been a big deal folkie back in Philadelphia pulled some strings to get us in a decent place there booked us at a joint he used to work at called the Bijou. Opening for some group I'd never heard of that I assumed were British called U2.

All the way down through New York and the Jersey Turnpike and over the river to Philly, we got a decent hotel and camped out. Band-mates discovered that the bars the allow beer take out and got shattered the night before in their rooms but I passed on that and passed out, only to rise at seven AM or so and wander, as I did. Just loved that city, the juxtaposition of the skyscrapers against the 1700's brick was even more pronounced than Boston was and the cheese steaks were as greasy fantastic as advertised and I had the best day as a Thrill perhaps of them all. Without the others, who smoked weed and watched soaps all day.

The reverie was washed away like a sandcastle at sound-check. U2 were set up and after a tuning, launched into their "I Will Follow" song, the one I knew and as me and the other Thrills (now actually called City Thrills due to a band on Long Island owning the name, when things turn to shit, oh do they turn) watched them, panic ensued. They sounded like the Who, all huge and vast and cavernous and clanging, only new and steady and stentorian serious. There would be no mopping the floor with these guys and so when our set came, Barb froze in fear. Plus, as Mike had been huffing herb all day, the tempos were molasses slow and he was too groovy to pick them up.

I didn't sit in a fucking van for 7 hours to die a death in the shitty of Brotherly Love only to fume all the way back up the Eastern Seaboard on the way back to Boston after being gawped at a la Mount Rushmore. I got as much leeway as I could out of my cable and hopped off the stage and started kicking over the tables, all of which had baskets of popcorn on them. Philadelphians are so tough, well prove it them--none of them moved a muscle. After the set, a few did come up to me to tell me that the band sucked but I was all right. The U2 guys were princes, too. And not Tea Bag Brit jerkoffs, but lovely Irish lads, no attitude, decent. But this was an abortion of a road-trip from the standpoint of playing music.

The center can't hold much longer, man.

MARCH 1982

I know it comes from an old poem but it is on endless loop rewind in my head--I'm a stranger and afraid in a world I never made.

All of our peer bands from our wave were gone or going. Richie's band, done and him too New Waving it with a surf band, LaPeste gone, their singer having reinvented himself as a would-be Gene Vincent and the Neighborhoods were burned out by a greedy manager that turned them into a mule team bar band, playing so often that their sets never changed. We too were at the end of the rope, rendered superficial by a double headed monster, disco now having morphed into what was called "synth-pop" to our right and to our left, this strange new amped up version of what we were doing in 1978, only much more crazed and meaner and all male testosterone bonding and bashing that was called "hardcore".

As I have nothing but bilious loathing for anything that's utterly static and lifeless as what I heard in the grooves now pounding out at the dance clubs, I had no affinity for this dull pulse. Yeah, like everyone else, I loved "Don't You Want Me Baby" and "Just Can't Get Enough" but it seemed almost like the 1910 Fruitgum Company mixed with Kraftwerk when it didn't work. Hardcore, on the other hand, was punk rock. And I loved it, as did Sean--rehearsals were now a few of our songs and then "Rise Above" and "Six Pack" and "Depression" by Black Flag, "Pay to Cum" by the Bad Brains, "Wasted" and "Red Tape" from Sean's faves the Circle Jerks and my absolute heart's devotion, "Ha Ha Ha" by my number one group of them all, Flipper. Mike tapped along amused but he and Barb were still of the mind that we should make a go of it radio hit wise-- especially after the massive success of the Go Go's and Blondie.

Merle, who knows what he thought. He wasn't saying. Not to me, anyway.

The hardcore kids themselves were a riot. In those shaved heads and chains and scarves on boots and that thing they magic-markered on their hands, the straight edge logo (while sucking down our beers in our dressing rooms and doing coke with us, I was liquor dry but still drug friendly), I found them to be the only signs of life, them and a crew of people that hung about at this new restaurant that opened above the Rat called the Hoodoo Barbeque. City Thrills was going nowhere, the only local rock band of any note was Mission of Burma and even they seemed like they may have peaked after their brain shattering single "Academy Fight Song" and the mega-mighty follow up "That's When I Reach For My Revolver".

Funniest to me was that the hardcore fellows (there were barely any females) had generally been Thrills fans and even roadies for us, including the presumptive ring leader of the cadre, Springa. A nonstop talking machine, Springa fronted the first and pretty much the best of those bands, SS Decontrol. Springa, a little, wiry blond kid from Quincy was like the younger brother everyone dreamed of—assuming that "beating the shit out of them daily" was part of the dream. This is not a knock—he could virtually segue from anything into anything—like a rant about the Red Sox into why Dez was a better singer than Henry for Black Flag—on a dime. In other words, one needed a bit of serenity to deal with him or one would wanna throttle him, lovable though he was. SSD sounded to me like a highly tightened tantrum in a washing machine or better, Van Halen at 400 mph without the showoff lead guitar, in fact, SSD's guitar player was the anti-Eddie Van Halen—never smiled or soloed and looked like one of the Bruins with guitar as hockey stick aimed at an imaginary puck and net. Their drummer was also from Wellesley and so I convinced Barb to book them with us at the Rat.

She did. Their crew rioted and the bouncers threw them out and Barb got fired as booker. Sorry, Toots.

They and GangGreen and the FU's and Negative FX and the Proletariat were the only exciting people left to see. And I was conscious enough to realize that we could never do that music convincingly, we knew too much, the scourge of maturity slammed that door shut.

So, I called the band together and spoke my piece. We were done in Boston. Nothing would ever make us hot stuff again baby in any evening. But we had a core of togetherness forged by four years of hard work and calling it a day would therefore be a total waste. Hence, my henchmen and hench-lady, we had to move.

"We gotta start over in New York", I said, scanning their eyes for a reaction. "We'd be fresh there. Who's in?"

Barb nodded as did Sean. Mike, I was worried about--he was married and had a proper gig and a house and was a settled down sort of laid back fellow probably not so prone to this great adventure. To my utter shock, he nodded.

Merle said nothing. A few weeks later, he called me, first time in a year. No, Johnny Angel, I am not going to New York. And hung up. I lost a coin toss with Sean, which meant I was gonna be the new bass player. I bought a cheap one with a metal neck and sat in front of my new chick Carole's stereo for hours, fingering along to the Pretenders and to old Bowie discs. Carole was an adoring 18 year old with a very swank place in Brookline, she never asked too many questions and found me endlessly amusing, whereas most of Boston found me just plain endless.

JUNE 1982
I kissed Carole goodbye, packed up my mom's station wagon, got Elissa (I was seeing both of them) and headed down I-95 to Manhattan. The new day had begun and we were gonna kick ass. And I made a mental note that I probably shouldn't have. I'm gonna look up Dee when I arrive.

Chapter 16/Baltimore MD/Facebook/ Cyberspace/October, 2013.

VIVDeMILO: Johnny??????
VIVDeMILO: Damn it, Johnny, they're about to board us any minute. Where the hell are you?
JOHNNYANGELWENDELL: Viv. What's up?
VIVDeMILO: Where have you been?
JOHNNYANGELWENDELL: Gym. Bootcamp. That lunatic Cuban had us do 200 burpees and 1,000 crunches. I'm standing on the verge of mass barf.

JOHNNYANGELWENDELL: What's up, you sound stressed.

VIVDeMILO: I'm at the airport in Baltimore.

JOHNNYANGELWENDELL: Trying out for the Orioles?

VIVDeMILO: Not funny and not now.

JOHNNYANGELWENDELL: Sorry...oh yeah--you saw McClain?

VIVDeMILO: I did. What a dreadful bastard.

JOHNNYANGELWENDELL: Did he Jesus the shit out of you?

VIVDeMILO: Not that badly, thankfully.

JOHNNYANGELWENDELL: Did you find Dee?

VIVDeMILO: Yes and no. I know more than I did and it isn't good, Johnny.

JOHNNYANGELWENDELL: She's dead?

VIVDeMILO: Yes.

JOHNNYANGELWENDELL: Oh fuck, I suspected as much. Shit. This sucks. How, where, when?

VIVDeMILO: He wouldn't tell me. It sounds like they disowned her. All I know is that she died at 27 and get this. Dee is not her name.

JOHNNYANGELWENDELL: ?

VIVDeMILO: Evelyn. Evelyn Monica McClain.

JOHNNYANGELWENDELL: Ugh. I can see why she changed it.

VIVDeMILO: He was such an asshole, Johnny. 'She turned her back on god', that's what that red-nosed pig actually said. I am so angry.

JOHNNYANGELWENDELL: Steady, baby, steady. Get home, cry yourself to sleep a few days and then Google her name again. Maybe check Social Security. Now that you know her real name, everything will open up, assuming you wanna keep going with this.

VIVDeMILO: I do. I have to know what happened to her. That family can't just pretend she never existed. I don't care about their pride, Johnny. This is so wrong.

JOHNNYANGELWENDELL: Well, then I gotta stand with you 100%, V. Meanwhile, I think I'll try to do the impossible myself.

VIVDeMILO: What is that?

JOHNNYANGELWENDELL: Cry. I can't. Masshole macho thing, I just get bottled up and it wells up like it is now and it burns away at me. I don't have to get the kids for a few hours, Wife working. Maybe I'll just take a walk somewhere and try to bawl a little.

VIVDeMILO: I think I'll do that after the flight, too.

JOHNNYANGELWENDELL: Keep me posted, kid. I kinda figured she had to be dead but it was something I didn't wanna ever accept, ya know. So many things I wanted to say, shit.

VIVDeMILO: I know, honey. Me, too. OK, they just told us to shut off all electronics.

JOHNNYANGELWENDELL: bye.

VIVDeMILO: Bye.

Chapter 17/Boston, Newbury Street/June, 1983.

Who says you can't go home again? I have and I did and I don't feel all that bad about at this moment because after a year on the wrong side of Hell's gates, all I can do is convalesce and gradually rise, from ass to elbows to heels to sea-sick vertical. Wobbly. But standing again anyway. Very, very tentatively.

Looking at the slanted shafts of light as they crash sideways into this deliberately dim-lit flat, I can get the motor going but it's gotta be quiet. This is because I'm temporarily cribbing with my overnight DJ laughing gas huffing buddy and he slides in around 7, which my internal clock plus the rising sun an hour ago tell me that was about 45 minutes ago. I have to ease out quietly into the daytime on this, my last and in fact only free day before resuming my on again off again career of the last six years minus the last one, the family brokerage business just outside Government Center.

I done surrendered and gave up and conceded to rejoin the straight world for one more go of it under the generally detached gaze of father and grandfather. But it was that or continue to flounder on the absolute bottom rung of the rusted and busted out ladder that was my life in Manhattan. I know when I'm beat and beat I was.

Got a minute? You'll need a shitload of 'em.

. . . .

It started out promising, the year that (City) Thrills was gonna finally wowie and zowie 'em by showing New York what a real, tight, taut rock and roll band was. Taking our cues from our betters and heroes the Heartbreakers, we did a series of farewell shows in Boston some 13 months back which raised at least a decent wad of cash cushion. The plan for that hiatus was to saturate all the bookers of the venues with our musical brilliance before we had to hunker down and get day work. Made sense to me.

But as is always the case with expecting things will go as you see them from a distance only to have them totally unravel up close, so did the great re-lo. First off, we didn't entirely know the lay of the land as it would influence our thinking-- in Boston, only one of us lived in a milieu unlike the others, so we tended to at least observe the same things on a daily basis. In Manhattan, we scattered--Mike was way uptown on 90th or so, East Side, Sean over near Chelsea, 26th and 8th, Barb near the UN on 48th and me, where I always seem to end up wherever I go, Bohemia--11th between 1st and 2nd.

That meant that what feedback and sway I got from below 14th St was a lot different than what filled their souls and ears. Plus, Barb's folks had money and Mike and Sean had mates. And as such, proper digs. Mr. A's modest place of residence was a pay by the week rooming house, with toilet in hall and shower adjacent. The building was strangely set up--half of it was on 11th, but my room was across a tiny courtyard in the back half. And the roof and edifice had that odd slant like half the place was already sinking into the East River. My neighbors were a serious step up in the eccentric department from the people I normally lived among in Massachusetts-- across the hall from me was a 70 year old guy with a crusty, cancerous growth across his left ear that literally looked like barnacles were eating his temple and covering the side of his veiny skull; every morning his ritual was to rise and clear out his throat loudly into the toilet for 15 minutes. What he hacked up out of those shattered and battered lungs of his, I can only imagine as 10 times as disgusting as the worst Secaucus waste not 20 miles across the Hudson.

Across the courtyard were two roommates from Bennington College, Jay and Rico and the super, Reggie. Jay was a smart-ass gentile and for a while my best pal in New York, Rico was a Jewish graffiti artist that snuck into subway yards and tunnels to create his carefully conceived pieces. I know this because I saw him draw them up before sauntering out to Long Island to shoplift the needed ingredient for these colorful and illegal murals, spray paint. He was very tight with the famous artists of the day and through him, I met the creme de la creme of the New York art world, like Keith Haring and even the savior himself, Andy Warhol.

Keith had a gallery opening with Andy in attendance and they served a roast pig on a spit. New York decadence!

Reggie the super was a different story. One of those "perpetually beaming, pumping out the warmth and sighing asides and sugary platitude type religious black folks that you take to immediately until they've conned you with their charm into doing some absurd favor for them" guys. Rico laughed his ass off when he saw Reg swindle a free move of furniture from his moms place in the Bronx down to the LES upon determining that I still had my mom's station wagon. That kind of solid favor is worth a bucket of ducats but out of town yokel that I was. It was all gratis. Never again. I am a quick study--quick enough to figure out the real Reggie wasn't the Bible thumbing, hosanna-proclaiming believer that hummed along to the Mighty Clouds of Joy on his box in the courtyard but in fact a zoned out heroin addict and boy-boinker. To get away with both of those trips means a lot of skill when it comes to working the marks and he'd honed his to rapier sharp.

Jay and Rico hated the band, mine that is. They thought we were corny and small time. Jay loved hardcore and Rico rap music. What we all loved-- we and the Italian numbers runners that collected on the stoop as well was "The Message" by

Grandmaster Flash, maybe the greatest record ever made. Rico and Jay and I bought it after hearing on late night radio once and popped that Sugar Hill sucker down for what had to be 20 plays in a row. My metamorphosis was beginning. This rap thing was stripped down and fierce like "Piss Factory" or "Little Johnny Jewel" were. I'd have never noticed this had I stayed in Boston because the idea that rapping was basically "black punk rock" would have been sneered out the door by my peers, most which didn't much like the sons and daughters of Africa.

See, it can never be said how night and day New York and Boston are. Boston may have its street tough Irish and in-fighting Italian mobsters and all, but the sheer fucking scale is so small, like the difference between a model airplane and an actual 747. Boston is quaint. No one would ever call my little corner of the city that, shit, one morning the numbers racket guys were all in full murmur mode because as a warning to their encroachment, a rival crew had deposited a severed, bloody head atop the garbage cans in front of the building. They scattered like Dee's roaches the evening of that day, never to be seen again.

Yes, despite Elissa's presence in the city (she got a place on 15th), I had Dee on the brain still. So much so, that I decided to leave her a note, which

I was scrawling out in the sunlight of the courtyard one afternoon when Reggie sauntered by.

"What you writing out, brother man, Johnny Angel?" he asked and I looked up to see his pupils a little less pinned than usual and some glide in his stride which meant he'd be antsy as shit shortly and so I better make sure my door was locked. He'd be on the Jones soon.

"A note to this rocker chick I knew in Boston, man", says me. And ducked my head down low as if to say "conversation over, motherfucker, I'm busy".

Even an abstract "no" was not gonna be taken for an answer. Haggling with the Puerto Ricans on 2nd and C for the H had upped his game in the worst way. "Yeah?" he asked. "Where she be at, then?"

"Chelsea".

Reggie scrunched his chin in hand and in contemplative thought and tilted his head beagle style at me.

"Black haired girl, real skinny, one of them punk rock girls?"

My jaw dropped. 2.5 million human beings in Manhattan and they know each other?

"That might be her," I reply.

Reggie reared back and laughed and let out a few theatrical coughs for effect, cleared his throat and said "Dee from Boston, right? Yeah, I ran with her a bit I did, she's around the way you know." He laughed again and slapped my back. "Dirty legs Dee from Avenue C. Yeah, I know her, she all right".

What the fuck was this goggle eyed, marionette like junkie scumbag queer on about, I thought. And I didn't like the jivey, put-down tone in his little serenade and I started thinking about crippling this plague of a semi-human being. But I'd already learned a valuable lesson from Rico as per New York street law--never rise to any bait, sit and wait. Let the other fucker play his hand and be the man.

"Well, man--if you see her tell her Reggie from 11th says hello. You can do that for me, right?" I nod in ascent.

"God bless you, Johnny--you got a good heart, man", And he ambled off to chew the ear off of whomever else was unfortunate enough to be at the end of however many bags he'd shot. I scribbled a few lines as I made sure he wasn't returning:

"Dee, baby--it's me, Johnny. I'm here now, we moved to New York. I'm at 320 E 11th St, 2E in the back. I got no phone yet. I love you, Johnny".

And off I walked, across town to her place. Name still on mailbox. No letters or flyers in it. I jammed my note in, hit her bell, waited, hit it again, nothing. And headed back to 11th Street.

....
....
....

We renamed ourselves again, this time "Untouchables NYC", after the TV show and added the NYC for cool effect and because we'd learned there was a ska band in LA with that name already. Armed with a new demo of much cruder and more street potent songs, we tried to get into the clubs like Danceteria and the Ritz and the Peppermint Lounge and Irving Plaza, but all were dry holes. The pull we had in Boston counted for nothing and all the old CB/Max's bands we used to play with were finished. The best we could do and did was to play the hardcore club A7 and we went down like the proverbial Titanic there--as small as the place was, the kids would jam into the other room to get away from us!

The only decent shows we'd get were in Connecticut via Sean's old peeps and even those were echo room empty. The best gig I had in that year was with our old friends and mentors, the Ramones, which I got by running into Johnny on the street and asking him if anyone was opening for them in Asbury Park, he gave me their road manager's number, I called and the great man himself, Monte put us on.

Like fathers like sons and daughters at that point, them and us. They too were seen as done, old hat. Their attempt to sell out with Phil Spector and 10CC people producing them had done little but wreck their rep like our little purple pop EP wrecked ours. But they were the mighty Ramones and filling the Fast Lane on a Friday night wasn't out of their ballpark.

Our shows with them had always been orgies of blurry energy, first the little guys and then the titans. But that was in friendly territory. No one on the Jersey shore had ever heard a quarter tone of us. So, three songs into our set, we paused and up came that droning, deadly chant--"hey ho, let's go, hey ho, let's go".

So that's how it is, you beach ball slime-buckets? Hoot me off the boards? I think not. I turned my bass all the way up and shouted in Barb's ear---

no more stops, same to Sean and indicated to Mike it was double time all the way out. And these wharf rat suburban bush league wannabe's got that we'd laid down the gauntlet and then they started surging the stage. Barb knocked a few back with her mic stand, Sean smacked the butt of his SG into another's head and Mike even took perfect aim and like William Tell, hit this one little twerp in the sinuses with a drumstick. Me, I stood and didn't react, like I did when bullies used to try and beat me in Wellesley. I don't even feel you little man--give it up.

After we closed with "Hey!", we had to part these grebos like the Red Sea to get to the dressing room and I figured here comes the bloody reprisals. Nope--nothing but back slaps and congrats, we were all right. The Ramones had to run through the same line of "hey man's" themselves, which set poor Dee Dee off. "I hate this fuckin' place", he said. "Everyone touches you".

And that was the crest. In all other things, life went completely dog-shit as fast as you could say "Lexington Ave. Express". Elissa went home to Florida with pneumonia and I blew off visiting her, not to mention blowing off my brother's wedding in Illinois. I was too out of it. Because alcohol and I had resumed our relationship, kicked in by Jay's constant prodding that I down forty-dogs with him.

I caved. Once that switch went on, there was no shutting it off. And now it was on every damned night, generally at this cheap Polish place on St Marks, the Holiday. Even as my savings dwindled, seven bucks meant seven drinks and then the Holiday would close early and maybe mosey somewhere else. That bar was ace---the regulars like the crazy hairdresser with a pistol in his boot and the hardcore kids and even Allen Ginsberg--all dropped in over a night's course and the great old 60's oldies on the juke--finally, a real home for me. Planted at the end of the bar was this one wildly dressed chick with her hair always up in a bonnet and always talking louder and gesticulating more vividly than anyone else and one night I asked Rico if he knew her, she was like a busted wire twisting on the pavement type exciting.

"She's a dancer chick, I hear", he said." From Michigan. I think her name's Madonna".

A few months later we heard her on the late night between Bambaataa and Rocker's Revenge singing "Everybody". Hometown pride, baby. I wish Barb could have absorbed whatever that girl had, because her energy level was at gutter level. And in New York, her habits went from nasty to lifestyle. But because I loved her as one does love one's best friend and she was mine--I enabled and that meant that she could use my sink to fix in, as her copping ground was in my hood and not hers.

I wouldn't ever recommend watching someone fix if you don't have to. The burning spoon, the stink, the draw and all that blood--and then the personality change from agitated to bliss that sounds almost attractive but isn't in person. But better in my safe place than in a burned out Avenue D tenement--at least here if she went out, I wouldn't let her die.

What did die in New York was the unspoken agreement we'd made at the beginning of the band that she and I would never cross that one last major line with each other. She was off-limits to all males in that band otherwise it couldn't work. And we did, after an entire afternoon of booze for me and booze and dope for her then off to the Holiday for cheapies. In the booth in the back, Barb--barely able to see--suggested the unimaginable. Which I was completely up for. The last pussy frontier, as it were.

My mind was. The rest of me, no. For one of the few times ever, my piece remained at peace, he wouldn't rise. It wasn't just the booze, looking back it had to be that deep down I knew that fucking her meant ending the band and I wasn't ready for that. But as if by reflex, it finally did work a little, pitifully and the deed was sadly accomplished.

The next day we were both coated in sweat, shock and shame. Gentleman that I can be, I rose enough to fetch a chicken Parmesan sub from the grinder-a-torium on 1st to split which neither of us could choke down, not to mention look at or speak to each other and she beat a hasty retreat to the street and cab and uptown. I couldn't help but wonder if she was now like every other female I knew, nothing special about her, no matter the wars we'd been through. If that's the case, the band is done and so are we.

A week later, a very angry landlord beat down my door at 5 AM on a Saturday--I owed him 800 bucks and he was coked to the gills up all night ruminating mode pissed off and ready to kill me. Not knowing I had any rights, I forked over all remaining cash and realized that what little I had coming in from my part time telemarketing job on 42nd would never cover. So I did the unthinkable —scrammed and crashed on the floor of the same woman I'd run from screaming in 1978! She'd been in New York a few years attempting to break into the fashion world. In the middle of the night, before that red-eyed freak of a landlord could padlock my meager stuff away, I vamoosed.

She was only a block away, across the playground on 12th. And I could pay no rent and drink and free wheel and philander but at the bottom of this bacchanalian well, there was a sense that there was no more road ahead for my true love, my first love and really my only love, my band.

I had gotten a construction gig up on 57th, building a new office for IRS Records, the same dildos that had nixed us at Hurrah's in '79 and the dough was starting to come in a bit. But it was back breaking exhausting labor hauling sheet rock and doing demo and getting faces and eyes full of gypsum every day and so when we did do gigs, sometimes I'd pass out in Mike's truck until right before set time.

The only place we had any pull was back in Boston, so occasionally we'd head up for a few shows. And they'd be pleasant enough, I'd shack with Carole and she had become a far more skillful partner in the art of oral in my absence, whose cock HAVE you been sucking, girl? But the shows were like nostalgia which I hated. We had one booked for first week of February and were practicing for it, with Barb playing rhythm guitar. I'd brought in a new song which we were knocking around whose hook was "hoping I see you soon/Lady Dee". Yep, no word from her, either. And after that rehearsal--no more band. As

I walked home to 12th Street afterwards, I knew we were finished. Even the very funny observation from one of the working girls on the street (I was wearing a skull and crossbones T shirt and she asked "are you poison, honey?") didn't make me lift my chin up. The lifelessness, the listless half-hearted go through the motions that sat on our heads like a pregnant octopus, I couldn't deny it any longer. First I phoned Mike as I knew he was feeling the same thing (a month earlier, I'd suggested to him we wear all red suits and play Motown oldies to his dismay and revulsion) and he agreed, Sean, too. Barb didn't take it so well.

"Are you fucking kidding me?" she screamed into the phone. "You'll leave me--you'll desert me? I wanted only one thing, one more show back home and you'll take that away from me? What am I gonna do now, did you even think of that? Fuck you, Johnny Angel, you asshole, really, FUCK YOU!"

And that was that. Five years and change. And I put on my leather and met Randy, my workmate and the best egg in New York and we drank Buds and shot pool at the Blue and Gold on 7th as Willie Nelson nasalled away on the box, "you were always on my miiind..." And I thought I'd be crushed and devastated and I'd cry like a baby but instead I beat Randy for the first and only time ever (I suspect pity) and sauntered home down these chilly streets to 12th and a corner of the floor--the death of Thrills was not the death of my world.

....

....

I joined a British synth pop band on bass for a month and tormented the fuck out of them. As I was now no longer the band leader, all my frustration and pent up rebuttals to the five years of whiny tantrum shit-fit wet diaper wailing of my former band-mates was doled out to these unsuspecting and undeserving Human League fans and I lasted one ignominious gig at the Mudd Club before I was tossed. And despite my rummy spending binges on the ignorant oil, I had finally saved enough dosh to share a one bedroom on the corner of 7th and B across from the park. Floor no more.

One night at some new dive catty-corner from my new place on the West side of Tompkins Square Park, I ran into my old friend, Barb's former lover and the Senders/Heartbreakers drummer Ty Stix. How out of the loop were we both, he didn't even know we'd been there nine months at that point. He was accompanied by this very pretty and somewhat familiar blond girl in a red leather who said almost nothing and sipped the same beer for an hour.

As I was splitting to conk out, Ty stops me and says that his friend wants to invite us over to watch slasher films with her. That is a whole lot more interesting than late night bad joke telly to me and she hails us a cab to her place on 10th. As we're let out at her door, it dawns on me how I do know her--this is Johnny Ramone's building and this is his girlfriend, Roxy.

Well, that sort of makes us family, doesn't it? Their apartment is perhaps half the size of mine, a small square box with one piece of furniture, a huge bed and at its feet, a state of the art television. How two people could live here in this space and not annihilate each other baffles me, it's barely bigger than a cell at Riker's really, no exaggeration. But Cynthia (her actual name and what she was introduced to me as) puts a film in the Betamax box and lets it roll, the great Herschel G. Lewis classic "2000 Maniacs".

It's almost "Rocky Horror" with her how she knows each scene and the moronic dialogue. But I am really enjoying its amateur idiocy a ton, more than Ty did, as he went right to the land of Nod halfway through, snoring away next to us. For perhaps a second as the film broke, Cynthia and I met eyes and being on a bed already anyway, started kissing each other with this wave of pent-up reddish glowing energy I'd never felt before--I hadn't made love to anyone since the band broke up and her man was on the road somewhere.

We vibed instantly. Cynthia was aggressive sexually, a 180 from her passive and stony silent verbal self at the bar. She slammed my hand hard down between her legs and ran her middle finger atop mine in exactly the spot and angle she desired and I was very pleased and impressed. But as much as I really was digging this demanding and imperious hand jive, I whispered to her that I couldn't fuck her with Ty sleeping next to us, I was sober. Craning my neck about, I saw that she had a little oven on a small level above and I motioned that we go over to it. Placing her lap on the lip of the appliance, with her ass maybe an inch from the burners, I took her legs under my arms, got up on my tippy toes and jammed Johnny Jr all the way into Roxyland. This soon got tiresome and we repaired to the bathroom where she gulped my battered swollen schlong as I sat on the edge of the potty. I've always had a tough go of it cumming from a blow job no matter how proficient the sucker may be, so we did stop to pause and talk. I asked her if this meant she had an "open relationship" with Johnny, I got no reply but a strong tug on my schlong and a resumption of the delightful dive. Oh, fuck this shit and Ty, we strolled to the bed and fucked madly for an hour, him not moving a blissed out muscle in the process.

I phoned her a few days later and we made a date in her little cell. When I arrived, she had her girl pal Gail with her, which I didn't like at all, but Gail soon scrammed and Cyn and I went at it unfettered by Ty or chaperone for hours. She explained afterwards that she had forgotten what I looked like and was afraid she'd bedded a Quasimodo. I, like the Beatles on the roof, however, had passed the audition.

We fucked constantly. Like every day and night. As I was in between jobs, I had the time and she had the money. I had become completely addicted to her and couldn't bear to be away from her, despite the fact that she was, for all intents and purposes, another man's woman or so I thought. A man that phoned every day and grilled her about the mail everyday--his thing was to send out to retired ball players and get their autographs and because he'd proffer a swap of his own signature scrawl, he got them.

I felt zero guilt about this situation. Cynthia gave me no reason to feel that way and if it was not a problem, I was damned well not gonna make it one out of misguided application of principle. We were happy--generally. When one's sex life is full-on psychotron, to keep it fueled means there must be corresponding amounts of fighting and did we ever. Plus, the Bird, as I called her (from her impressive platinum plume) liked to fight a lot--especially if she got smacked, she really loved to be hurt. This did run counter to my way of thinking, I'd always regarded men that hit women as subhuman turd slabs. But she loved it and frankly, I loved her. Not only did I oblige with many an open palm, so did I develop a genuine taste for her flesh, that meaty pale rump of hers was purple, black and blue from all my chomping. Which, when she was shitfaced (and generally she was), she'd proudly display to whomever visited the pad by dropping her panties.

Eventually, I descended enough off my pink love cloud to realize that I didn't get anything out of even the most casual sadism and to her credit, she was cool about my refusal to throw anymore blows.

Maybe it was the box-life confines of her dungeon that created this scene, I don't know, but when we did venture out one afternoon to hang out with a sax-playing, "No Wave" ex of hers with a particularly loathsome rep to shoot coke, I had finally maxed out on the drama and trauma. I motored up First Avenue with her on my heels, the cut in the crook of her arm still fresh from the shot, me hoping to outpace her. We ended up on the floor of the Avenue B chateau having particularly vicious make-up sex anyway. I was strung out on the Bird like Barb was on the smack.

But as Barb was being elbowed out as number one woman in my life by the yellow-headed masochist, we still decided to attempt to work out our differences over a few bottles of two buck Chuck in the tiny kitchen at Avenue B. My roomie was back in SF with his mom and pop, Cynthia was back in her bird's cage watching films and eating dum dum noodles and Barb and I had the night to maybe set things straight.

Of course, drinking oneself into oblivion is the least likely highway to resolution but it's the one we'd always driven on and so we drank and threw recriminations and blame back and forth like it was a tennis match. "You did this to me", "well, you did that to me", volley, volley, volley. And in circles and getting more mush mouthed and blithering to boot. As the volume went up as the wine went down, somewhere in the brain of Barb it must have seemed like a good idea to really let me know how she felt with one particularly demented gesture. With one quick motion, she picked up the empty wine bottle and slammed me upside my head, the butt end connecting with my cheek.

I can't get hit in the face. That is the trigger into a spiral of out of control reprisal when sober, let alone shit-faced and in my house and after countless weeks of S/M role-playing with Bird. And even if you're 300 pounds of muscle, my face gets creased by blow, it's kamikaze time and always has been. I first felt a wave of total humiliation and schoolyard embarrassment that this pipsqueak whom I outweighed by a good sixty pounds would even dare it but that lasted less than a four count. She got a straight right back to the chops and when she landed arse first on the cracked linoleum of the kitchen floor, the bottom of my right boot sent her whole body horizontal. As red-eyed lit as she was, she was now in abject terror that I was gonna kill her and a plea for clemency via sex was the only way out.

"Johnny, Johnny, listen, "she panted out, "I'll fuck you, OK, let's go to your bed, let's fuck, all right. That's what you really want, isn't it, just don't kill me."

I wanted to vomit. Not even atop her head as a kind of ultimate fuck you salute from my stomach, just so turned off and disgusted, I couldn't answer. Best friend to me? No, I felt as flat and as trod upon at that moment as what I'd always really been to her, a stepping stone. I strode over to the door, opened it and pointed to the hall. As she raced to what she thought was safety, I cursed her out. "Run for it, you useless junkie skank. Get the fuck out of my life and never fucking come back".

As I sit on Albert's floor and recount this craziness, I feel waves of nausea slapping me like high tide. I hate myself for ever raising my fists on her. However cruel she was, she didn't deserve that in the least. And it wasn't like Bird's S/M games where she deep throats me after a wailing, it was just plain horrible and psychotic.

I didn't get the option of apology, though. She beat it to her dealer's on Avenue D no doubt to calm her jagged nerves. Me, I was monomaniacal--to the Bird's nest and shaking and seething the whole way past the park and up to 10th and over.

When I arrive, Cyn let me in and immediately sensed that the volatility was not a prelude to a pussy pounding as it usually hinted at. I was raving insanely at all the way up volume and no matter what she did, I kept accelerating. I was gonna kill that woman, she hit me? Finally, she suggested I phone my brother who was in law school, he'd tell me what the repercussions would be. Coolly and calmly all the way from Chicago, my little brother talked me off the killing ledge.

And I broke down. And started sobbing like an infant. "How could she do this to me, Bird?" I asked, over and over, my head on her breasts and her stroking my hair and telling me all would be all right. "How could she do this to ME?"

....
....
The Ramones' tour of spring 1983 was winding its way east and that indicated that the carrying on would have to slow down. I dreaded my playmate being removed from my clutch like I dreaded cavity fillings. That was weighing me down, that and the worst straight job I have ever had and hopefully will never have again.

Unemployment on Manhattan was at 12 plus percent in Reagan's recession and no one was hiring. Occasionally I'd get something like moving my friend Wayne Kramer into his new place with his new wife in Tribeca, which paid for a week of supplies. But there was nothing and rent was due and Bird feeding me was not gonna placate the new landlord. As it happened I ran into an old college pal of mine, Eddie B. at CB's one night and I laid my sob story on him. Turned out that post grad, he did what I always did when the well was dry--went to work for his father. Difference being, my dad was a stockbroker and his dad ran this horrible chatka warehouse on Broadway called Norman's House of Deals.

Charles Dickens in his wildest Shepard's Pie fueled nightmares could never have imagined this repellent den of atrocity. All day hauling crates of badly made in Japan useless trinkets onto pallets or onto trucks until the mind numbing routine made you seek sanctuary, which meant basically trying to find a nook or cranny anywhere away from the banal chatter of Norman's (Eddie's dad's) chimpanzee-like cronies. Basically, there was our clique of punk and pop musician types like me, Chris who played bass and was also an Emersonian, Hoy Boy, a lanky, wry cat that sang and sometimes when he could get out from under dad's evil eye, Eddie himself. The others reminded me of my own dad's foul smelling, cigar chomping racetrack tout sleaze-ball, middle aged Jewish roustabout laggards. And they dogged my ass day in and day out and laughed their asses off when the Bird would drop by for lunch in her Lolita/whore ensemble. Probably out of jealousy that this tottering shiksa was gleefully emptying my nuts as they had to make do with their own greasy fists, eat your hearts out, landsmen.

Small consolation. The pay was forty in cash a day, six days a week. And I could not tolerate the lunk-head deal at Norman's with Cynthia demanding all night super service clit twiddling. The former being exhausting miserable and the latter being exhausting exhilarating. Meaning I was getting maybe five hours a night's sleep. That meant artificial energy and so along with every other malady, I was now popping trucker's candy every morning like vitamins.

One day, the speed plus fear of an impending end to the Bird romps got me. A boom box was clipped off the back of a truck out front. And Norman was livid and knew that Eddie would protect me, so being helpless in the matter of a shit-canning which might alienate his already antsy son (Eddie hated the place as much as we all did and was way too brilliant to be slinging shit his whole life), Norman decided a little humiliation was in order--handed me a broom and told me to sweep out the showroom. And as I pushed it back and forth, I saw a limo cruise slow down Broadway and realized, if I stay here, I have no chance at one of those, except on the way to the cemetery. I dropped the broom, said nothing and walked the 18 blocks to the Bird's.

She let me in and I looked into her eyes and she smiled calmly. Having just returned from a week in detox, she was wonderful--I have never seen anyone with a drinking issue like hers, a spoonful of cough syrup with a hint of alcohol would turn her purple and babbling. Today, that wasn't an issue and so I asked her--besides you, is there any reason I should stay in New York?

She shook her head slowly and said nothing. There was no debate. To celebrate, we decided to get Indian down on 6th at the Green Door and walked arm in arm proud over to Second Avenue and as we crossed Seventh Street I saw a familiar looking guy, a short black man half hunched over the gutter, bent and pretzel-like. He looked up at me as I was checking him out and smiled broadly at us.

"Johnny Angel", he said and coughed the cough of a death rattle that doubled him back over. Cynthia stepped back cautiously and I made a gesture to assure her we were OK, or he was, anyway. It was Reggie. But even though he was a dark-skinned man, I noticed that there were these grotesque, purple, bruise-looking splotches on his face and scalp, like an odd sort of frazzled mask or maybe bloody patches of skull were tearing through his skin. He asked me if I had maybe some change and I handed him a dollar, got a "God bless" and a half mast wave goodbye and I guided the Bird to Chicken Vindaloo and peace a block away.

That was two weeks ago. We packed up my stuff and came north and made love one more time on my floor. And I drove her back to Manhattan and came home to Boston alone, with "Come On, Eileen" blaring out of every station along the way.

And I sit here on Albert's floor, next to the burn marks our tanks of Nitrous made a few years ago and I strum out this new song I started thinking about, about Thrills and Dee. It's got this sweet, Drifters, "Under the Boardwalk" lilt and it goes like this:

"I walk a lonely avenue/nimble ballet, cause I got holes in my shoes/oh, pins and needles on the sidewalk/when winter finally cedes to spring/and we can speak of better things/maybe we can set aside the cruel talk/Lookin' back on you, baby doll, you were the/best love I ever had/looking back on you baby doll, you were the/sweetest thing I ever had/oh, no no no".

I guess you could say that I loved New York rock and roll a lot more than it loved me, right?

Chapter 18/Facebook/Jacksonville FL/ Cyberspace/October, 2013.

VIVDeMILO: Johnny?
VIVDeMILO: Johnny, come on. I know you must be online, you always are.
JOHNNYANGELWENDELL: Viv.
JOHNNYANGELWENDELL: VIV. OK, I gotta eat, ping me later
VIVDeMILO: Johnny, are you there?
JOHNNYANGELWENDELL: There you are. I assume you have news?

VIVDeMILO: Yes. Lots. None really good. I hope you're ready.

JOHNNYANGELWENDELL: Yeah. Lay it on me. What do we know?

VIVDeMILO: I found her father's obit. "Randall McClain, 85, former sales VP, Goodyear Tire. Survived by his loving wife Dorothy and sons Robert and Randall Jr., predeceased by daughter Evelyn. Services at Holy Sepulchre Cemetery, Saturday, April 14th at 11AM, Rochester NY. In lieu of flowers a donation is suggested to Catholic Charities of Rochester".

JOHNNYANGELWENDELL: We knew all of that from the wrong reverend Mouthpiece McClain already.

VIVDeMILO: Yes, but I assumed that they had a family burial plot there and so I did a graves search for Dee there.

JOHNNYANGELWENDELL: Is that where she is?

VIVDeMILO: She is. Her stone says "Evelyn Monica McClain, RN Beloved daughter. Sleeping in the arms of the holy-spirit. 1956-1984".

JOHNNYANGELWENDELL: "RN Beloved daughter. Sleeping in the arms of the holy spirit"? Good thing she's not alive to see that.

VIVDeMILO: Oh, I don't know. She did go to Catholic schools as a kid, she may have been religious.

JOHNNYANGELWENDELL: More like wishful thinking on the part of her fucking parents. In death, she could be what they wanted her to be, in life, seems like she wasn't.

VIVDeMILO: Don't be angry, Johnny.

JOHNNYANGELWENDELL: I'm not angry at all. I'm a parent and I get it. We wish our children would be the spitting image of our fantasies and dreams. But you gotta accept them as they are. She hated that name, clearly. I reckon she'd have hated that pious god bullshit, too.

VIVDeMILO: Maybe.

JOHNNYANGELWENDELL: So, this is it, I never hear from you again. Case closed?

VIVDeMILO: Is that what you want?

JOHNNYANGELWENDELL: No. I wanna see you. Your dedication to keeping this faith alive has floored me, Viv. And I wanna say goodbye to Dee. Not motherfucking Evelyn, Dee.

VIVDeMILO: So we should have our own ceremony?

JOHNNYANGELWENDELL: Exactamundo. I got frequent flyers, I can book a flight to Buffalo. You down?

VIVDeMILO: I am. I was going to ask you the same thing.

JOHNNYANGELWENDELL: Two weeks maybe--- you got any shoots?

VIVDeMILO: Let me check.

VIVDeMILO: Two weeks from Saturday, I have three days off.

VIVDeMILO: OK?

JOHNNYANGELWENDELL: I can be there. I'll red-eye it that Friday and get to Holy Sepulveda late the next afternoon.

VIVDeMILO: Sepulchre.

JOHNNYANGELWENDELL: LOL, yeah. Can
JOHNNYANGELWENDELL: t blame that one on Auto Correct.

VIVDeMILO: lol, no.

JOHNNYANGELWENDELL: It's a date. Not a particularly fun one but a date all the same.

VIVDeMILO: I think we should put on our old punk rock stuff for Dee, don't you?

JOHNNYANGELWENDELL: Good idea, I'm down. But you may wanna skip the fishnets, weather wise, V.

VIVDeMILO: LOL--so true. You do think of everything, my dear. Let's call it a go and stay in touch until?

JOHNNYANGELWENDELL: Done. I'll see ya.

VIVDeMILO: bye.

Chapter 19/Rochester NY/December, 2013.

I can't imagine in my wildest dreams wanting to live here in Rochester, New York nor would I wanna spend eternity in death here, either. That knife-blade sharp keening wind off Lake Ontario that can find any unguarded patch of skin no mattered how layered you are, the omnipresent gloom, the gateway to the dying "Rust Belt", Valhalla it ain't. I hope that this, my first time here is also my last.

Not to mention that getting to this little bit of Hades South of Canada was a bitch to end all bitches. A red-eye to Buffalo, as it so happens, is over a grand and frequent flyer miles don't apply on the routes. All flights from LA to Toronto and New York City were booked on this eve of Dee's two person ceremony and so I was forced to fly into Boston and drive the Pike and Thruway ten plus miserable hours here.

Viv came in a day early to see her beloved cousins in Massachusetts and has already gotten a motel room a mile from the cemetery. I'll pay my respects and do the immediate turnaround and stay with a former band-mate from a different crew, he's in Revere, ten minutes from Logan in Boston. And then back to LA pronto--my distaste for this end of the country is the worst kept secret in the world, my aim is to be laid to rest far, far away from the place of my origin. I will not spend thirty extra seconds in the Northeast if I don't have to.

Pulling my rental through the gates of this Holy Sepulchre Cemetery manages to do the nearly impossible. As shitty as I felt about the brutally boring haul as it took Ativan popped down like Pez just to get on the metal bird in the first place, the boneyard has actually bottomed out my mood a few feet deeper. That and the post-benzo bummer and jet lag are making my eye lids sag like sewer lids. The bare, barren lay of this place make the above ground as lifeless as the interred below. Dee, baby--I know you never knew how much I loved you when you were alive, if you could only imagine what it took to get here. As the narrator of that great old Elvis (Costello) tune "Oliver's Army" would say, I'd rather be anywhere else than here today.

Dee's grave is around a slight hillock to my left and after negotiating the tiny curve, I see one small white sedan pulled over the side of the road, which I presume has got to be Viv's. No back of blond head over the driver's seat as far as I can tell by peering through the back window, pulling up. She's probably already here--it's quarter to four and the short winter sunlight is about to end. She's likely been here for a while.

Pulling over on this muddy little strip and going around the front of the car, I can see Viv--first time ever, but I know it's her, blond lady in black leg-warmers and spiky heels with a biker jacket pulled over a fuzzy, striped sweater, crouched over Dee's modest headstone laid flat into the earth. Say what you will about we aged punkers, we got style--same jacket for me, pegged black jeans (real ones, not those ridiculous "Strokes/hipsters" drain-pipes that the unicycle riding, ratty topped locals presently adore in Silver Lake), the same engineer boots I bought with the Bird in Manhattan, the steel toes almost peeking out through the worn out tips and the soles skinnier than a slice of New York provolone.

"Hey, Viv--I'm here".

Viv stands up and turns around and my first thought is, fifteen years in Florida and still "underside of the trout" pale, just like me. Curious, we ran to the lands of the sun only to stay out of same at all costs. We of Northern European stock burn and wrinkle easy, though.

She turns to toddle down the tiny rise to meet me and as I can now make out her features, her eyes are puffed red and edged with ring of tears. And she throws her arms over my shoulders and I can feel her heaving against me, that kind of unstoppable hysterical pulse that my kids get when they're overwhelmed.

"Let me take a look at this thing, K?" And she nods, takes my hand and leads me to a small, level bit of carefully manicured earth now more tundra than grass. Evelyn/Dee's stone is maybe 18 inches by 10 inches and her name and inscription is barely legible, tiny gold trim and lettering and a somber black gloss of a stone.

I do not cry. I can't, there's an internal governor that raises its palm and stops me before I get there. I didn't cry at my own father's funeral, nor any of my grandparents. I am shut down and repressed, me, the supposed wild man of uninhibited emotional outbursts in public and I can't mourn aloud. Don't ever get the idea that this is a point of pride in manliness, it is 100% pure cowardice--I can't bear for anyone to see me as a hurt little boy.

But seeing her marker set deep in this cold, cold ground in a city she hated next to a father that disowned her (I assume) and thinking of her as a lonely battered junkie going out for the last time in the stinking mist of an Avenue D dawn or worse, the wave of sorrow capsizes my ship and I have to turn my head away from Viv so she doesn't see me breakdown. But Viv's a woman and they know--she circles her arms around me as I look down, both of us cemetery silent.

I free myself from her embrace and kneel.

"Baby, it's me, it's Johnny. I know you can't hear me, I know you're not here and I know I'm talking for me and not you. If you only knew....yeah, if you only knew how much I loved you, would that have made any kind of difference at all? Did I let you down? I'm so sorry, baby--if I'd left that bitch for you and been honest and true, we'd be together, I know". I stop here and look away for a moment as reality is singing loudly. I love my family. I know I'm just letting it out now and it's all right.

Gently, I run my fingers over her name on the stone. "Evelyn. Fuck that shit, you're Dee, my lady Dee and always will be. You remade yourself and if only this battering ram shit-house world of ours hadn't run you over, if that fucking weasel Rowland hadn't sent you down the drug line, you'd be walking with us now, maybe in LA, maybe in Florida, I dunno, but baby--you checked out too soon, if you only knew what you missed" And on "missed", I lose it and start sobbing and shaking and Viv kneels down beside me.

"He's right, Dee. We were wrong about growing old (irony of ironies being that I boasted to Dee in her Chelsea flat with stupid youthful pride that I would not make it to 30 and she chastised me for such a moronic rodomontade), I hope you're resting easy or maybe, I have no idea, rocking it with Stiv or Johnny Thunders or Sid somewhere"...her voice tails off and she looks at me.

"That was kind of silly, forgive me". And I shake my head like everything is fine, the evening has landed on us, it's cold and we're bent out of shape.

"It's cool, Viv. I have no prayers or words. Just so sorry you aren't here, by now you'd have been an RN for thirty years, looking back on all the people you helped heal. Baby, I got nothing left for you. Nothing"

And I stand and look at Viv. And she me and we hug each other sideways like and I pause and I ask her if I'm right.

"About what"?

"Rowland". I almost spit out that sicko's name like cancer phlegm on the frozen earth. "Viv, Dee was just a silly, fun-loving party girl until that pervert dosed her. After that, she was damaged goods. Everything went to shit after that one night, the runaway to Manhattan, the OD's, the addiction, the disappearance. That baby-raping fuck stick gossiping on Facebook, he's never suffered a single minute for this, that motherfucker".

Viv nods. "I can't dispute that, Johnny. But I think your anger is just a way to push your grief aside. Maybe a little angry at Dee, too?"

And Viv kneels back down and rubs Dee's stone clean with the sleeve of her sweater and bends over to kiss the letters of her name. And turns her head to me as if to say it's your turn as well, and so I kneel and bend down and kiss that freezing block and try to make my mind believe it's Dee's soft warm chops and it's 64th Street and we're in love with the panorama of possibilities that are just waiting for us like ripe peaches on a branch.

And I can feel Dee's fingers caressing the back my head, running through my hair but no, those are Viv's. Still beside me kneeling, she looks at my eyes and sighs a little smile and whispers out in her halting way, can I be your Dee, Johnny?

We move our faces together in the arctic gloaming and lightly kiss and then both of my lips are over her top lip and then bottom one and I pull her under me, Deeply sucking her tongue and she mine, running my palms through her scalp, wanting to crawl right into her brain, wanting mine to stop talking and just let go. I jam my nose into the side of her neck and bite her ear lobe in my eyeteeth and she lets out this gasp almost a hiccup and slams her tongue into my ear and as she removes it, she pulses out a few disjointed sounds, moans and pants that seem to be words but are this hum, this din. And she opens her legs and pulls my hips into hers and as her skirt slides down and her sweater up, the exposed strip of her skin touches the frigid surface of Dee's gravestone and she reflexively arches up. I take off my jacket and slide it under her ass so she doesn't get the same shock and also maybe to shield Dee in some peculiar fashion from this most bizarre turn of events.

And the mist of our breath is dropping on our faces in the arctic stillness of an Upstate winter's day, giving the impression of sweat and bringing back that very first time with Dee and only at that moment does my mind stop chattering out its warnings and I am more than good with its silence.

Viv has undone my jeans and is stroking my cock hard through my briefs, as carried away as we are into this madness, her hands are not yet warm enough to do anything but recoil me. I am doing the same to her, in that tiny space between her leggings and panties, the side of my hands is running a steady, engine like caress across the top of her neatly shaved pussy. With one quick tug, I pull her cotton undies down and she kicks back her feet to let them fly off onto the ground, then slides both her hands down the sides of my legs to bring my briefs down enough to expose me and with those same hands now on my bare ass, pulls me into her with one deft, hard stroke.

All I can see is the stars over her shoulder and this blazing red arc of blood pumping in my face is all I feel as she is bucking me back as hard as I thrust down upon her. She is moaning that speaking in tongues abandoned gurgle as her head is tilted to the side and then she turns to face me, the whipping wind sending a tear across her face like the first drops of a storm across a windshield.

"Call me Dee, John. Call me her name".

"Dee, baby Dee, I love you so much Dee, come on and love me back don't go baby, please," I gasp out and Viv is now pulling my hair and digging her nails into the bottom of my back as we writhe in this freezing, deserted goddamned fucking cemetery atop my former lover's dead body. And time stops and the wind pauses or maybe it didn't and I just stopped feeling it but Viv is moving slower and no longer writhing but slowing me down consciously, I can feel her pussy pulsing on her heartbeat and she looks at me with a face that is blank, it signifies whatever I want it to mean to me, I know it and she takes a deep breath and tells me it's time, Dee wants you to cum now, please cum inside her.

And I push as far as I can go into Viv or Dee or Viv's body and Dee's soul, the confusion is a damned maelstrom now and her hips buck back as if to snap and sap every drop of me out of me and into her. And I do and as we look at each other, Viv smiles up at me.

"Follow me to my hotel, I hope they haven't lock these darned gates already, let's hurry".

And we turn from each other and collect ourselves and pat our pockets for our keys but I noticed her and she me making one last glance at the temporarily warmer bit of green and brown ground that will lay forever above her, Evelyn Monica McClain.

Chapter 20/Rochester, New York/December 2013.

I haven't had a drink in 28 years and change. I gave it up on the last day of August 1985 about three years after my persistent drunk of an upstairs neighbor on the Lower East Side got me back on the slosh-train. DOA was playing the Rat, I drank 12 beers in an hour, went home with a girl not my sweetie and realized that I could no longer continue this mad dash to cirrhosis. But I know a hangover when I feel one and this is damned close, it's almost to a hangover what an O'Doul's is to a beer---awfully close to the real thing. I don't know where I am, mouth is dry, body feels beat and it takes a dozen deep breaths with eyes wide open to get any semblance of bearing.

I am in upstate New York in a motel in Rochester. I fucked a woman I met yesterday for the first time after 30 minutes together atop the tomb of my most deeply unrequited love and did it cold sober, very cold, given the month and place. The clammy trickle of panic sweat is rolling down to the small of my back--this one, if it gets out, could never be explained away to anyone, especially Mrs. A.

Instinctively, I reach for the bottle of tranks in my bag. Screw that nonsense, I have a flight to catch in some 15 hours or so. No time to slow down.

And no Viv. Or a note. How polite of her. Given that we had resumed the twisted role playing begun at Holy Sepulchre here in this dingy suite not two minutes after arriving here, I'd say she owes me at least a chat. But that too can wait, maybe she had an earlier flight and given the distorted fun house mirror of a romp we had yesterday, I can't begrudge her an early departure sans goodbye.

I gotta sit and plan out my course of action, first to explain how I was a late night no-show in Revere. That's easy. But I just can't concentrate for shit, something is eating away at me and it doesn't feel like infidelity guilt. I gotta get my body in gear.

Brushing the grunge off my morning choppers, I am one disheveled and sad sight in the mirror, looking more balding and five o'clock shadowed than ever, just a middle aged dumbbell that regressed all the way to 11th Grade last night and I got this sickly carnival melody on tape loop circulating in my head. That happens a lot and always has, signals a song idea usually, but this one is nauseating, like a nursery rhyme from a horror flick, no words, just that merry go round oompah that makes you wanna slam your palm into your forehead till it stops.

And then I feel it. Sister Panic Attack has arrived unannounced. This freezing cold shiver blast up my left side from my face down my arm and to the top of my leg and I look at my forearm and all the hair is standing up and my calves are wobbling and now the melody's got words and it's being sung by that twisted little junkie bitch Reggie and it gets louder on every refrain.

"Dirty Legs Dee, from Avenue C, Dirty Legs Dee from Avenue C, Ha ha ha, ho ho ho", now it's Flipper's song and then back to Reggie and my knees go and it's a "bone-crusher", the worst kind of Level 10 panic where all you can do is lie on the cold tiles of a bathroom and wait for the jackhammer slam and dizziness and nausea to pass you by like the Angel of Death on Passover. They're sudden and incredibly violet. I hate these, they're unanticipated and so untreatable and I pull myself up and lean into the can in case I have to vomit. I'm a long way from LA, which scares me even more and I can feel my soul spiraling ever downward. Freezing rivulets of sweat on my brows and a twitch I can't stop and then all goes silent in my head and as if a neon sign is flashing away, I get it. My head clears. The thoughts are now clean and linear and I can push myself vertical on the toilet to standing. Breathing normally and tom-tom boom atomic bomb of my heartbeat is now a gentle snare volley, nice and slow. Clarity.

Years ago, I wrote columns for the LA Weekly about crime and one of my subjects was a Mexican Mafia assassin from the San Gabriel Valley. He said in an aside that he had sired a daughter with a streetwalker from Monterey

Park--a woman he called "one of the Garvey Avenue dirty legs".

Dirty legs. A hooker. Dee was a hooker. Not just a trust fund baby that came to an unfortunate end, an all the way, all out, down at the bottom of the barrel 3rd Avenue denizen of the world's oldest trade (that's where they worked, I assume junkie Reggie called her Avenue C as the place they copped together). I remember staggering home on 12th more than a few nights to see those girls blowing the newspaper delivery men in the cabs of their trucks and feeling nothing but rage for a world that dropped such degradation on people whose only recourse was to barter time for orgasms and money from these vile men. And now I started to re-feel the rage that was brewing in my gut yesterday at the cemetery.

If it wasn't an OD, it was AIDS. That time and Reggie's bruises and that they ran together means needle sharing. And her place of death according to Viv was here in Rochester. That means my sweet baby either wasted away to nothing, covered in hideous disfigurement or slammed the shit one last time in a suicide run here in the sticks. That mental picture makes me yelp a bit and I have to bite down on my tongue and hard. That knowing, baby cherub face with its toothy grin all contorted and drawn and now I can picture her in her box up the road. Bones. A box with baby's bones. Shaking a little, no I can't do this again. So I start a breathing count, four in, four to hold, four to exhale so as not to panic again. And the clarity returns as well.

Rowland. Motherfucking Nick Rowland, that third rate, pasty little wisp of a degenerate pig, he had to push the button that sent her into this nightmare abyss. I'm a drug addict and drunk too and I blame me for it, but I was shoving the shit into myself voluntarily, that sick cocksucker poisoned Dee out of some fractured jealousy over a guy that wouldn't have given him the time of day if he was the last option in the universe. And now I can feel this rage starting to build and spill and get louder inside my head like an oncoming division of tanks over a hillside, guns blazing.

Because Dee is but one of the many in my life. After I moved to Los Angeles and was safely out of sight from the day to day in Boston, I started to get regular emails and calls from many of my old running buddies in the band scene. They all began the same, the "how are you" catch up, but it would turn--as I was away, I could be trusted with this thing that had been eating away at them since they were kids and because for all of my earned rep as a prankster incarnate, grade-A, blunt spoken asshole, I was also thought of as righteous, a man of my word. And each of them-- male and female--would open up and spill it out.

How this priest or this minister or this teacher or cop or relative insinuated themselves into their sphere past appropriate and that their first sex was with a preying Praying Mantis adult, an innocence stealing, ice-veined, purple lipped pervert. How they gave head to a grunting creep in a cassock in the confessional or behind an equipment shed at school or in a holding cell, picked up on a dirt weed charge and I could feel the shame and agony or read it in their emails and texts and tell them it was not going to kill them--it was done, it's gone, we're grown, we can let this shit go if we don't hurt anyone, bring love wherever you can. Yeah, that's New Age, Hallmark card sounding maple syrup simpletonia, but it's also true.

And the sweats have stopped, I notice and I can stand completely straight again and after a few glasses of metallic, putrid tap water, I'm human. And it occurs to me that other than Viv and my wife, no one knows I'm here, in fact, the Revere blow off can be explained as I never went in the first place.

Which means I am invisible. And an invisible man can go anywhere and do anything.

Like even it up for Dee. And Billy and Linda and all the others. I can't avenge them all, but I know where to start. I think it's time Mr. Rowland and Judgment Day got better acquainted by me.

....
....

One thing about mama's boys is that they never leave home if they don't have to and I can't even count the number of those that I know never left her place. It isn't like Nick Rowland was gonna marry and have kids, even if the same sex deal becomes legal in the MA, that isn't his thing unless NAMBLA takes over the Lege and as nutty as the politics of the state are, that isn't even worth mulling over as a sci-fi fantasy. He's gotta be psychically tied to her apron strings, they always are.

I figure I have a window of maybe two hours to deliver the beating from hell onto this fucker's head, scram to the airport and get to California in safety. However badly I smack him around, I know enough to know that the reminder to him that I am well aware of his proclivities is enough to get the sick little bastard to keep completely quiet and take this like a man and yes, I am aware of the implication of how revolting that sounded.

I hate violence. I deplore it, it is sickening. But just once--fucking once--a kid fucker is going to get a payback. And this particular pedophile poisoned an innocent and for all intents and purposes, murdered her slowly. I have to be careful that I don't accidentally murder him fast.

Google Maps and Zillow tell me that this stately if weathered white Newtonville house I'm in front of is the same address as mommy dear's. As I pull up, I check the app for her Social Security. Deceased, 1993. And there's only one car, a beat up 2002 Volvo in the driveway. If he's here, he's alone or better, in the act--that will double his panic and triple the likeliness of him keeping his trap shut.

I so hope that's his and him. I slide a glove onto my right hand, one of the pair that genius boy left in the car at Holy Sepulchre, good thing Viv and I did the humpty dance or I might have had frostbite. I'll knock with the right, no DNA, when he opens the door, shove his ass down on the floor and drive straight rights into his kisser until no one can recognize him and then boot-scoot out to Logan. Not like it matters if there's any evidence. A text a few days later reminding him that I know his secret and that was only the beginning unless he accepts the punishment I just meted out.

Now or never. Park, make sure no one's walking a dog or whatever and stride fast to the front door and get this over with. I imagine Dee on my shoulder rooting me on like Ali against Joe Frazier. Up the creaking steps to the door and to knock.

Fuck me, why is it open--in December? What the fuck is wrong with this twisted old shit, is part of his trip freezing? I push it ajar a bit and look to the dining room to the left, down the narrow hall to the kitchen, no sounds, and then over to the living room which is set down a few steps. I walk over and look down at his sofa and figuratively, I freeze.

At the foot of the worn out, burgundy couch, splayed out akimbo is the now formerly living Nick Rowland. That same gross, pasty complexion, only waxen and still and the darting scheming eyes static. Not moving and those beady eyes open. Palms open, fingers out and as I walk to beside him, I see an empty plastic bottle next to his head. No sign of struggle, no blood, nothing. And this is no heart attack, someone's been here, otherwise the door wouldn't be open.

And I feel that chill again from this morning and my hairs rise and I start to breathe way too fast-- can't have a bone crusher here, I turn and elbow the door open, look both ways up and down his street, no cars, no people and run like a track star to the car. Popping the keys into the ignition, I realize I don't have a lot of time.

....

....

....

First time I came back to Boston in eight years away was in 04, to do a band reunion with the group I had after Thrills, the Blackjacks. Was a lovely time all the way around, but when you've been away a long time, you notice things the locals overlook, as it's their day to day.

Namely, that the little berg had nightmarish big city traffic everywhere, even out in Wellesley. Took forever to get anywhere, especially the airport, even first thing on a Sunday morning and now it was dinnertime, Saturday. Shit, onto the Pike, into that Big Dig thing, I am Dale Earnhardt--I gotta get to Logan and way quicker than post haste.

Through the shiny Sumner Tunnel and into Eastie, past Santarpaio's and I don't even have time to return the rental. I'll park it in the garage and leave it, call them in a few hours and claim it's stolen, it'll be found a few days later, no harm, no foul. Leave the keys in it but on the floor to be extra convincing, I didn't write about crime for years without learning a few tricks of the trade. Racing across the street in front of the terminals, I start checking the flights for any headed to

Jacksonville. Delta's got one leaving in 45 minutes, gate's maybe a five minute quick walk and I would wager my life's savings, she's getting ready to board that fucker for the sunshine state.

As I approach, I slow down and get behind a group of businessmen so as to be unseen until the very last moment. They're sauntering nice and slow and I pretend to be looking the other way, they have no idea they're Johnny-shields. If they only knew.

And there she is, that shiny blond mane over winter leather and skirt, only the slightest variation on yesterday's fuck me ensemble in Rochester. Back turned to me, perfect. I ease around the suits, and from behind her, I tap her lightly on her shoulder.

Viv turns and backs up, semi-startled. And I look into her eyes and tip my head ever so slightly and ask what's been brewing in my head for the last hour.

"How'd you get him to drink it, Viv"?

At first she bucks back on her heels a little, as if to give the wheels in her head time to lie or concoct one fast. But you can't con a con, not here, not in Florida, nowhere. I know what happened, I wanna know how it did happen. This doesn't seem like the timid little Viv I'd just gotten to know, on the other hand, her reserve online hadn't prepared me for our tete a tete atop the tomb, either.

She's cornered and to make any scene would be a fatal error and she is nothing if not calculating and fast. This whoosh of tranquility falls off her eyebrows like morning dew and she smiles knowingly and ever so slightly.

"I told him it was two bullets in the brain or drink the GHB, Johnny. His choice."

"Where the fuck did you find a gun in Massachusetts on a winter Saturday?"

Now she was beaming. Looking left to right, she fixed her peepers upon the same face she'd been sitting on not 18 hours ago and bared her gleaming pearlies.

"Toys R Us, Johnny. Where else?" She was proud of it. And as a matter of (literal) execution, I guess I was proud of her, too. Good show and all that.

I needed ask nothing else as I shook my head and tried not to smile, I had to at least appear flabbergasted. The drug she procured from a body builder she knew from her photo-shoots, that I figured out on the way over. As GHB is a recreational drug, the cops would assume that Queen Nick huffed the dose not knowing it was in fact 25 doses. Rowland, carrying a lifetime of abuse on his hunched, caved in little back was easy to fool in the gloaming of a winter's day with a toy gun, the asshole was pushing 70 and probably could barely see. All I wondered was if her voice did that trailing off thing as she offered up his choice of execution.

"No. I told him I was dosing him like Dee and he'd be sick a few days. He believed me, I think he was so relieved I didn't shoot him, he bought it".

"Are you going to turn me in, Johnny?"

And I didn't even have to think about it. I shook my head no.

"It goes to my grave with me, Viv", I said. "Just do me one favor, promise?"

"Yes?"

"Don't fuck anyone on it, all right?"

And she threw back her head and laughed and knew there was nothing else to talk about. She merely beat me to the scene of a crime I never committed and in my gratitude, my silence was assured. I kissed her forehead and patted her shoulder.

"Baby, you done real good. Not legal for sure, but good. Some things don't appear to be right at first, well, I was thinking about it all the way over and I realized that all of life is a war, not just on battlefields and sometimes wars get ugly. This was war, V. And now it's over".

"You really believe what I did was right?" she asked and I shook my head no.

"No, good and right aren't the same thing. I don't know what's right but in this instance, you did a good thing. As long as that sick schtrudze was vertical, he was probably getting kids horizontal, Viv. I'm no vigilante or supporter of them usually, but the world—our world, the world of Massachusetts when we were growing up—was truly and seriously fucked up and you moved it towards sanity maybe just a tick, but in the right direction anyway". And I leaned over and kissed her flushed cheeks.

"Don't worry about me, kid and don't be ashamed, k?"

She shut her eyes and nodded, opened them again and stared at me.

"Life goes on, right?" She asks. Yes, I responded, it does. Case closed, door slammed, final word, gavel slammed down. And all I can do is nod myself. It's done and over.

And I turned and waved and said that we'd text soon maybe, yeah? She nodded and the intercom announced boarding and with that she winked and got in line.

I have a flight of my own to catch. I don't ever want to see these walls again, not ever. Not ever.

Chapter 21/Facebook/Cyberspace/February 2014.

VIVDeMILO: Hey rockstar!

JOHNNYANGELWENDELL: Hey photog. Que pasa?

VIVDeMILO: Not too much. I saw your post--you're playing today?

JOHNNYANGELWENDELL: Yes ma'am. Right up the street, the Thirsty Crow.

VIVDeMILO: I saw. Good place?

JOHNNYANGELWENDELL: It'll do. We like it, me, Robbie and the boys.

VIVDeMILO: That's good. I like your new stuff, you're still funny, old fellow--you still have it.

JOHNNYANGELWENDELL: Whatever it is, thanks.

JOHNNYANGELWENDELL: You working?

VIVDeMILO: Yes, a "history walk" a "winter garden special" and Jacksonville's first ever same sex wedding!

JOHNNYANGELWENDELL: Say hi to the crazy fundies for me--if you know what I mean.

VIVDeMILO: I do. There won't be any there, this place isn't THAT backwards.

JOHNNYANGELWENDELL: I'll have to take your word for it.

VIVDeMILO: LOL, I know. Johnny, I have to thank you. Without you, this thing with Dee would never have resolved. I didn't realize how awry it would go or ever expected what happened to happen, but I feel so much better that it's over.

JOHNNYANGELWENDELL: I feel the same. It's done, she can rest or maybe we can.

VIVDeMILO: I agree. I do have to ask you one last favor if you don't mind.
JOHNNYANGELWENDELL: Go for it.
VIVDeMILO: Could you guys play "Hey!" tonight? Not for me.
VIVDeMILO: For Dee.

THE END

EPILOGUE

No one goes through this life in a straight line. Cradle to grave is not a razor's edge, it's a slide out of mama and from there on in, every person that you meet is like a shove in a hazing line at a Frat Rush or a gang initiation. You get jostled by them, your family, your teachers, your friends, those people you compete against or meet or sleep with. Everybody has some effect on you. How much they do--individually--is what makes us what we are. We're the sum of our experiences and acquaintances.

Dee and Barb and Sean, now gone and way too early, took those shoves and prodding and pushing like they were somehow an insult and battered back against them instead of just accepting them as part of the journey and to keep on going. I miss them because I figure that we were all born around the same time, we all walked the same boulevards in our choices, it stands to reason that we should end up at the finish line together, too. Reason isn't part of the equation, of course. Dee was too young to even have a past and the others kept doing the unproductive parts of their existences, maybe they believed that if they kept acting like they were 21, they'd be 21 forever.

Last year, I wrote this tune called "New York Dolls" about my favorite group and in the first verse, I wrote that "people make shrines of their past that become their prison cells" and I meant it in the way that so many of us revere our carefree adolescence and our twenties like they were unique to us. And no one else can ever feel our special feelings because our time was the best and you'll never understand because you didn't live it. But that's thinking with self-imposed blinders on, all days are good and bad, young or old for everyone. I don't wanna be forever trapped in my history like the poor mastodons glued to the goo of the La Brea Tarpits, rotting away where they stood. No thanks.

And never get the idea that I would glorify Dee because she "lived fast and died young and stayed pretty for eternity". That romantic view of early passing mixed in with the self-pitying arrogance of the survivor, that's that "People Who Died" bullshit. Never from me ever. The tragic and salaciously recounted passing of a Billie Holiday or a Johnny Thunders or an Elliott Smith is dimwitted, their deaths weren't glorious and beautiful, and the music is as it lives after they died. I'd like to believe that my take on them and my deceased comrades is the only one that matters.

But that's my own arrogance talking, my sense of importance and my belief that I took the beatings, physical and psychic and kept going, why didn't they, all my heroes and friends? Because they ain't me and I ain't them and I'm not better or worse, just lucky, really. Fates and chance and lack of order rule the day and I have been one truly fortunate son here. I could be nestled in an urn on my wife's mantle but as you can tell, I am not.

Unless I get hit by a bus tomorrow in which case I take it all back.

Soldier on.

Johnny, February, 2015.